STAND OUT

Evidence-Based Learning for College and Career Readiness

4

THIRD EDITION

STACI JOHNSON

ROB JENKINS

NATIONAL GEOGRAPHIC LEARNING

CENGAGE Learning

Australia • Brazil • Mexico • Singapore • United Kingdom • United States

Stand Out 4: Evidence-Based Learning for College and Career Readiness, Third Edition
Staci Johnson and Rob Jenkins

Publisher: Sherrise Roehr

Executive Editor: Sarah Kenney

Senior Development Editor: Margarita Matte

Development Editor: Lewis Thompson

Director of Global Marketing: Ian Martin

Executive Marketing Manager: Ben Rivera

Product Marketing Manager: Dalia Bravo

Director of Content and Media Production:
  Michael Burggren

Production Manager: Daisy Sosa

Media Researcher: Leila Hishmeh

Senior Print Buyer: Mary Beth Hennebury

Cover and Interior Designer:
  Brenda Carmichael

Composition: Lumina

Cover Image: Jade/Getty Images

Bottom Images: (Left to Right) Jay B Sauceda/
  Getty Images; Tripod/Getty Images;
  Portra Images/Getty Images; Portra Images/
  Getty Images; Mark Edward Atkinson/
  Tracey Lee/Getty Images; James Porter/
  Getty Images; Dear Blue/Getty Images; Seth
  Joel/Getty Images; LWA/Larry Williams/
  Getty Images; Dimitri Otis/Getty Images

For product information and technology assistance, contact us at
Cengage Learning Customer & Sales Support, 1-800-354-9706

For permission to use material from this text or product,
submit all requests online at **cengage.com/permissions**

Further permissions questions can be emailed to
permissionrequest@cengage.com

Student Book
ISBN 13: 978-1-305-65559-1

National Geographic Learning/Cengage Learning
20 Channel Center Street
Boston, MA 02210
USA

Cengage Learning is a leading provider of customized learning solutions with office locations around the globe, including Singapore, the United Kingdom, Australia, Mexico, Brazil, and Japan. Locate your local office at
www.cengage.com/global

Cengage Learning products are represented in Canada by Nelson Education, Ltd.

Visit National Geographic Learning online at **NGL.Cengage.com**
Visit our corporate website at **www.cengage.com**

Printed in the United States of America
Print Number: 04   Print Year: 2018

ACKNOWLEDGMENTS

Ellen Albano
Mcfatter Technical College, Davie, FL

Esther Anaya-Garcia
Glendale Community College, Glendale, AZ

Carol Bellamy
Prince George's Community College, Largo, MD

Gail Bier
Atlantic Technical College, Coconut Creek, FL

Kathryn Black
Myrtle Beach Family Learning Center, Myrtle Beach, SC

Claudia Brantley
College of Southern Nevada, Las Vegas, NV

Dr. Joan-Yvette Campbell
Lindsey Hopkins Technical College, Miami, FL

Maria Carmen Iglesias
Miami Senior Adult Educational Center, Miami, FL

Lee Chen
Palomar College, San Marcos, CA

Casey Cahill
Atlantic Technical College, Coconut Creek, FL

Maria Dillehay
Burien Job Training and Education Center, Goodwill, Seattle, WA

Irene Fjaerestad
Olympic College, Bremerton, WA

Eleanor Forfang-Brockman
Tarrant County College, Fort Worth, Texas

Jesse Galdamez
San Bernardino Adult School, San Bernardino, CA

Anna Garoz
Lindsey Hopkins Technical Education Center, Miami, FL

Maria Gutierrez
Miami Sunset Adult, Miami, FL

Noel Hernandez
Palm Beach County Public Schools, Palm Beach County, FL

Kathleen Hiscock
Portland Adult Education, Portland, ME

Frantz Jean-Louis
The English Center, Miami, FL

Annette Johnson
Sheridan Technical College, Hollywood, FL

Ginger Karaway
Gateway Technical College, Kenosha, WI

Judy Martin-Hall
Indian River State College, Fort Pierce, FL

Toni Molinaro
Dixie Hollins Adult Education Center, St Petersburg, FL

Tracey Person
Cape Cod Community College, Hyannis, MA

Celina Paula
Miami-Dade County Public Schools, Miami, FL

Veronica Pavon-Baker
Miami Beach Adult, Miami, FL

Ileana Perez
Robert Morgan Technical College, Miami, FL

Neeta Rancourt
Atlantic Technical College, Coconut Creek, FL

Brenda Roland
Joliet Junior College, Joliet, IL

Hidelisa Sampson
Las Vegas Urban League, Las Vegas, NV

Lisa Schick
James Madison University, Harrisonburg, VA

Rob Sheppard
Quincy Asian Resources, Quincy, MA

Sydney Silver
Burien Job Training and Education Center, Goodwill, Seattle, WA

Teresa Tamarit
Miami Senior Adult Educational Center, Miami, FL

Cristina Urena
Atlantic Technical College, Fort Lauderdale, FL

Pamela Jo Wilson
Palm Beach County Public Schools, Palm Beach County, FL

ABOUT THE AUTHORS

Staci Johnson

Ever since I can remember, I've been fascinated with other cultures and languages. I love to travel and every place I go, the first thing I want to do is meet the people, learn their language, and understand their culture. Becoming an ESL teacher was a perfect way to turn what I love to do into my profession. There's nothing more incredible than the exchange of teaching and learning from one another that goes on in an ESL classroom. And there's nothing more rewarding than helping a student succeed.

Rob Jenkins

I love teaching. I love to see the expressions on my students' faces when the light goes on and their eyes show such sincere joy of learning. I knew the first time I stepped into an ESL classroom that this is where I needed to be and I have never questioned that resolution. I have worked in business, sales, and publishing, and I've found challenge in all, but nothing can compare to the satisfaction of reaching people in such a personal way.

Along with the inclusion of National Geographic content, the third edition of **Stand Out** boasts several innovations. In response to initiatives regarding the development of more complexity with reading and encouraging students to interact more with reading texts, we are proud to introduce new rich reading sections that allow students to discuss topics relevant to a global society. We have also introduced new National Geographic videos that complement the life-skill videos **Stand Out** introduced in the second edition and which are now integrated into the student books. We don't stop there; **Stand Out** has even more activities that require critical and creative thinking that serve to maximize learning and prepare students for the future. The third edition also has online workbooks. **Stand Out** was the first mainstream ESL textbook for adults to introduce a lesson plan format, hundreds of customizable worksheets, and project-based instruction. The third edition expands on these features in its mission to provide rich learning opportunities that can be exploited in different ways. We believe that with the innovative approach that made **Stand Out** a leader from its inception, the many new features, and the new look, programs, teachers, and students will find great success!

Stand Out Mission Statement:

Our goal is to give students challenging opportunities to be successful in their language-learning experience so they develop confidence and become independent lifelong learners.

TO THE TEACHER

ABOUT THE SERIES

The **Stand Out** series is designed to facilitate *active* learning within life-skill settings that lead students to career and academic pathways. Each student book and its supplemental components in the six-level series expose students to competency areas most useful and essential for newcomers with careful treatment of level-appropriate but challenging materials. Students grow academically by developing essential literacy and critical-thinking skills that will help them find personal success in a changing and dynamic world.

THE STAND OUT PHILOSOPHY

Integrated Skills

In each of the five lessons of every unit, skills are introduced as they might be in real language use. They are in context and not separated into different sections of the unit. We believe that for real communication to occur, the classroom should mirror real life as much as possible.

Objective Driven Activities

Every lesson in **Stand Out** is driven by a performance objective. These objectives have been carefully selected to ensure they are measurable, accessible to students at their particular level, and relevant to students and their lives. Good objectives lead to effective learning. Effective objectives also lead to appropriate self, student, and program assessment which is increasingly required by state and federal mandates.

Lesson Plan Sequencing

Stand Out follows an established sequence of activities that provides students with the tools they need to have in order to practice and apply the skills required in the objective. A pioneer in Adult Education for introducing the Madeline Hunter WIPPEA lesson plan model into textbooks, **Stand Out** continues to provide a clear and easy-to-follow system for presenting and developing English language skills. The WIPPEA model follows six steps:

- **W**arm up and Review
- **I**ntroduction
- **P**resentation
- **P**ractice
- **E**valuation
- **A**pplication

Learning And Acquisition

In **Stand Out**, the recycling of skills is emphasized. Students must learn and practice the same skills multiple times in various contexts to actually acquire them. Practicing a skill one time is rarely sufficient for acquisition and rarely addresses diverse student needs and learning styles.

Critical Thinking

Critical thinking has been defined in various ways and sometimes so broadly that any activity could be classified to meet the criteria. To be clear and to draw attention to the strong critical thinking activities in **Stand Out,** we define these activities as *tasks that require learners to think deeper than the superficial vocabulary and meaning.* Activities such as ranking, making predictions, analyzing, or solving problems demand that students think beyond the surface. Critical thinking is highlighted throughout so the instructor can be confident that effective learning is going on.

Learner-Centered, Cooperative, and Communicative Activities

Stand Out provides ample opportunities for students to develop interpersonal skills and to practice new vocabulary through graphic organizers and charts like Venn diagrams, graphs, classifying charts, and mind maps. The lesson planners provide learner-centered approaches in every lesson. Students are asked to rank items, make decisions, and negotiate amongst other things.

Dialogues are used to prepare students for these activities in the low levels and fewer dialogues are used at the higher levels where students have already acquired the vocabulary and rudimentary conversation skills.

Activities should provide opportunities for students to speak in near authentic settings so they have confidence to perform outside the classroom. This does not mean that dialogues and other mechanical activities are not used to prepare students for cooperative activities, but these mechanical activities do not foster conversation. They merely provide the first tools students need to go beyond mimicry.

Assessment

Instructors and students should have a clear understanding of what is being taught and what is expected. In **Stand Out**, objectives are clearly stated so that target skills can be effectively assessed throughout.

Formative assessments are essential. Pre- and post-assessments can be given for units or sections of the book through ExamView®—a program that makes developing tests easy and effective. These tests can be created to appear like standardized tests, which are important for funding and to help students prepare.

Finally, *learner logs* allow students to self-assess, document progress, and identify areas that might require additional attention.

SUPPLEMENTAL COMPONENTS

The **Stand Out** series is a comprehensive tool for all student needs. There is no need to look any further than the resources offered.

Stand Out Lesson Planners

The lesson planners go beyond merely describing activities in the student book by providing teacher support, ideas, and guidance for the entire class period.

- **Standards correlations** for **CCRS, CASAS,** and **SCANS** are identified for each lesson.
- **Pacing Guides** help with planning by giving instructors suggested durations for each activity and a selection of activities for different class lengths.
- **Teacher Tips** provide point-of-use pedagogical comments and best practices.
- **At-A-Glance Lesson Openers** provide the instructor with everything that will be taught in a particular lesson. Elements include the agenda, the goal, grammar, pronunciation, academic strategies, critical thinking elements, correlations to standards, and resources.
- **Suggested Activities** go beyond what is shown in the text providing teachers with ideas that will stimulate them to come up with their own.
- **Listening Scripts** are integrated into the unit pages for easy access.

Stand Out Workbook

The workbook in the third edition takes the popular **Stand Out Grammar Challenge** and expands it to include vocabulary building, life-skill development, and grammar practice associated directly with each lesson in the student book.

Stand Out Online Workbook

One of the most important innovations in the third edition of **Stand Out** is the online workbook. This workbook provides unique activities that are closely related to the student book and gives students opportunities to have access to audio and video.

The online workbook provides opportunities for students to practice and improve digital literacy skills essential for 21st century learners. These skills are essential for standardized computer and online testing. Scores in these tests will improve when students can concentrate on the content and not so much on the technology.

Activity Bank

The activity bank is an online feature that provides several hundred multilevel worksheets per level to enhance the already rich materials available through **Stand Out**.

DVD Program

The **Stand Out Lifeskills Video Program** continues to be available with eight episodes per level; however, now the worksheets are part of the student books with additional help in the lesson planners.

New to the third edition of **Stand Out** are two National Geographic videos per level. Each video is accompanied by four pages of instruction and activities with support in the lesson planners.

ExamView®

ExamView® is a program that provides customizable test banks and allows instructors to make lesson, unit, and program tests quickly.

STANDARDS AND CORRELATIONS

Stand Out is the pioneer in establishing a foundation of standards within each unit and through every objective. The standards movement in the United States is as dominant today as it was when **Stand Out** was first published. Schools and programs must be aware of ongoing local and federal initiatives and make attempts to meet ever-changing requirements.

In the first edition of **Stand Out**, we identified direct correlations to SCANS, EFF, and CASAS standards. *The Secretary's Commission on Achieving Necessary Skills,* or SCANS, and *Equipped for the Future,* or EFF, standards are still important and are identified in every lesson of **Stand Out**. These skills include the basic skills, interpersonal skills, and problem-solving skills necessary to be successful in the workplace, in school, and in the community. **Stand Out** was also developed with a thorough understanding of objectives established by the *Comprehensive Adult Student Assessment Systems* or CASAS. Many programs have experienced great success with their CASAS scores using **Stand Out**, and these objectives continue to be reflected in the third edition.

Today, a new emphasis on critical thinking and complexity has swept the nation. Students are expected to think for themselves more now than ever before. They must also interact with reading texts at a higher level. These new standards and expectations are highly visible in the third edition and include *College and Career Readiness Standards*.

Stand Out offers a complete set of correlations online for all standards to demonstrate how closely we align with state and federal guidelines.

IMPORTANT INNOVATIONS IN THE THIRD EDITION

New Look
Although the third edition of **Stand Out** boasts the same lesson plan format and task-based activities that made it one of the most popular books in adult education, it now has an updated look with the addition of National Geographic content, which will capture the attention of the instructor and every student.

Critical Thinking
With the advent of new federal and state initiatives, teachers need to be confident that students will use critical-thinking skills when learning. This has always been a goal in **Stand Out**, but now those opportunities are highlighted in each lesson.

College And Career Readiness Skills
These skills are also identified by critical thinking strategies and academic-related activities, which are found throughout **Stand Out**. New to the third edition is a special reading section in each unit that challenges students and encourages them to develop reading strategies within a rich National Geographic environment.

Stand Out Workbook
The print workbook is now more extensive and complete with vocabulary, life skills, and grammar activities to round out any program. Many instructors might find these pages ideal for homework, but they of course can be used for additional practice within the classroom.

Media And Online Support
Media and online support includes audio, video, online workbooks, presentation tools, multi-level worksheets, ExamView®, and standards correlations.

CONTENTS

Numeracy/ Academic Skills	CCRS	SCANS	CASAS
• Writing a paragraph • Comparing and contrasting • Setting goals • Using a bar graph	RI5, RI7, W1, W4, W5, W7, W8, SL1, SL2, SL6, L4, L5	**Many SCAN and EFF skills are incorporated in this unit with an emphasis on:** • Understanding systems • Decision making	**1:** 0.1.2; 0.1.4; 0.2.1; 0.2.2 **2:** 0.2.1; 7.2.6 **3:** 0.1.2, 0.1.6, 0.2.1, 7.1.1
• Active reading • Focused listening • Writing a paragraph • Brainstorming • Using context clues • Using an outline • Comparing and contrasting • Reviewing	RI1, RI2, RI3, RI4, RI7, RI8, W2, W3, W4, W5, W6, SL1, SL2, SL3, L1, L2, L3, L5	**Many SCAN and EFF skills are incorporated in this unit with an emphasis on:** • Allocating time • Understanding systems • Applying technology to task • Responsibility • Self management • Writing • Decision making	**1:** 0.1.2, 0.2.4 **2:** 7.1.1, 7.1.2, 7.1.3, 7.2.5, 7.2.6 **3:** 7.1.1, 7.1.2, 7.1.3, 7.2.5, 7.2.6 **4:** 0.1.5, 7.4.1, 7.4.3, 7.4.5 **5:** 7.4.2 **R:** 7.2.1 **TP:** 4.8.1., 4.8.5., 4.8.6.
• Comparing and contrasting • Writing a business letter • Active reading • Focused listening • Calculating budgets • Reviewing	RI1, RI2, RI3, RI4, RI7, W1, W2, W4, W5, W6, W7, W9, SL1, SL2, SL4, L1, L2, L3, L5		**Many SCAN skills are incorporated in this unit with an emphasis on:** • Responsibility • Participating as a member of a team • Acquiring and evaluating information • Organizing and maintaining information • Decision making

CONTENTS

Numeracy/ Academic Skills	CCRS	SCANS	CASAS
• Pronunciation: Rising and Falling intonation • Active reading • Focused listening • Reading a bar graph • Sequencing • Writing about preferences • Summarizing a process • Comparing and contrasting • Using context clues • Reviewing	RI1, RI2, RI3, RI4, RI6, W1, W2, W4, W5, W7, SL1, SL2, SL3, SL6, L1, L2, L3, L4	**Many SCAN skills are incorporated in this unit with an emphasis on:** • Allocating money • Understanding systems • Monitoring and correcting performance • Interpreting and communicating information • Reading • Writing • Decision making	**1:** 1.4.1, 1.4.2 **2:** 1.4.2, 7.2.7 **3:** 1.4.4, 1.5.3 **4:** 1.5.1, 6.0.3, 6.0l.5, 6.1.1, 6.1.2 **5:** 1.4.7 **R:** 7.2.1 **TP:** 4.8.1, 4.8.5, 4.8.6.
• Pronunciation: Euniciation and Intonation • Focused listening • Making inferences • Reviewing	RI1, RI2, RI3, RI4, RI7, W2, W4, W5, W7, W8, SL1, SL2, SL3, SL4, L1, L2, L3, L5	**Many SCAN skills are incorporated in this unit with an emphasis on**: • Understanding systems • Interpreting and communicating information • Writing • Decision making • Seeing things in the mind's eye	**1:** 0.1.2 **2:** 1.8.5, 2.5.6 **3:** 2.2.1, 2.2.5 **4:** 7.2.6 **5:** 7.2.2 **R:** 7.2.1 **TP:** 4.8.1, 4.8.5, 4.8.6
• Focused listening • Active reading • Using a bar graph • Calculating percentages • Skimming • Reviewing	RI1, RI2, RI3, RI4, RI7, RI10, W2, W4, W5, W7, SL1, SL2, SL3, SL4, L1, L2, L3, L5	**Many SCAN skills are incorporated in this unit with an emphasis on:** • Understanding systems • Self management • Acquiring and evaluating information • Interpreting and communicating information	**1:** 3.1.1, 3.1.3, 3.2.1 **2:** 3.1.1 **3:** 3.4.2, 3.5.9 **4:** 3.5.1, 3.5.3, 3.5.5 3.5.9, 6.7.3 **5:** 3.5.9 **R:** 7.2.1 **TP:** 4.8.1, 4.8.5, 4.8.6.

CONTENTS

Numeracy/ Academic Skills	CCRS	SCANS	CASAS
• Active reading • Focused listening • Writing a resume • Writing a cover letter • Reviewing	RI1, RI2, RI3, RI4, RI5, RI7, W2, W4, W5, W6, W7, W8, W9, SL1, SL2, SL3, SL4, SL6, L1, L2, L5	**Many SCAN skills are incorporated in this unit with an emphasis on:** • Self-esteem • Sociability • Acquiring and evaluating information • Speaking • Decision making	**1:** 4.1.8 **2:** 4.1.9 **3:** 4.1.3 **4:** 4.1.2 **5:** 4.1.5, 4.1.7 **R:** 7.2.1 **TP:** 4.8.1, 4.8.5, 4.8.6.
• Focused listening • Active reading • Reading a flowchart • Writing a description of a situation • Reviewing	RI1, RI2, RI3, RI4, RI7, W1, W2, W3, W4, W5, W6, SL1, SL3, L1, L2	**Many SCAN skills are incorporated in this unit with an emphasis on:** • Understanding systems • Participating as a member of a team • Acquiring and evaluating information	**1:** 4.1.9, 4.4.1 **2:** 4.2.1, 4.4.3 **3:** 4.2.1 **4:** 4.3.3, 4.3.4, 4.5.1 **5:** 4.4.1, 4.6.1 **R:** 7.2.1 **TP:** 4.8.1, 4.8.5, 4.8.6
• Focused listening • Active reading • Writing a paragraph • Writing a speech • Reading a flowchart • Writing a letter to a local official • Reviewing	RI1, RI4, RI7, W1, W2, W4, W5, W6, W9, SL1, SL2, SL3, SL4, L1, L2, L4, L5	**Many SCAN skills are incorporated in this unit with an emphasis on:** • Listening • Speaking • Responsibility • Self-esteem	**1:** 5.1.6 **2:** 5.1.4, 5.1.6 **3:** 5.1.4, 5.2.1 **4:** 5.5.7, 5.5.8 **5:** 5.1.6 **R:** 7.2.1 **TP:** 4.8.1, 4.8.5, 4.8.6.

For other national and state specific standards, please visit: **www.NGL.Cengage.com/SO3**

INTRODUCING

STAND OUT, Third Edition!

Stand Out is a six-level, standards-based ESL series for adult education with a proven track record of successful results. The new edition of *Stand Out* continues to provide students with the foundations and tools needed to achieve success in life, college, and career.

Stand Out now integrates real-world content from National Geographic

UNIT 1

Balancing Your Life

UNIT OUTCOMES
- Analyze and create schedules
- Identify goals and obstacles and suggest solutions
- Write about a personal goal
- Analyze study habits
- Manage time

Look at the photo and answer the questions.
1. What do you think the people are doing?
2. What activities do you do every day?
3. What do you want to do in the future?

Construction workers on beams at the top of the Stratosphere Tower in Las Vegas.

- *Stand Out* now integrates high-interest, real-world content from National Geographic which enhances its proven approach to lesson planning and instruction. A stunning National Geographic image at the beginning of each unit introduces the theme and engages learners in meaningful conversations right from the start.

Stand Out supports college and career readiness

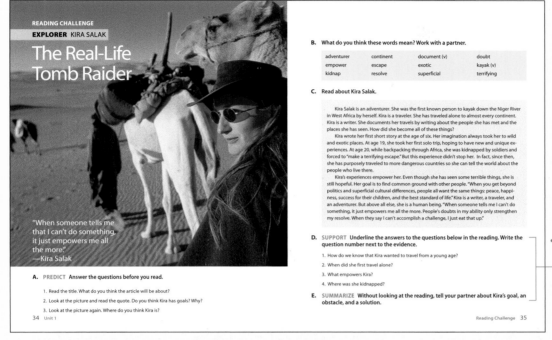

READING CHALLENGE

EXPLORER KIRA SALAK

The Real-Life Tomb Raider

"When someone tells me that I can't do something, it just empowers me all the more."
—Kira Salak

A. PREDICT Answer the questions before you read.

1. Read the title. What do you think the article will be about?

2. Look at the picture and read the quote. Do you think Kira has goals? Why?

3. Look at the picture again. Where do you think Kira is?

34   Unit 1

B. What do you think these words mean? Work with a partner.

adventurer	continent	document (v)	doubt
empower	escape	exotic	kayak (v)
kidnap	resolve	superficial	terrifying

C. Read about Kira Salak.

Kira Salak is an adventurer. She was the first known person to kayak down the Niger River in West Africa by herself. Kira is a traveler. She has traveled alone to almost every continent. Kira is a writer. She documents her travels by writing about the people she has met and the places she has seen. How did she become all of these things?

Kira wrote her first short story at the age of six. Her imagination always took her to wild and exotic places. At age 19, she took her first solo trip, hoping to have new and unique experiences. At age 20, while backpacking through Africa, she was kidnapped by soldiers and forced to "make a terrifying escape." But this experience didn't stop her. In fact, since then, she has purposely traveled to more dangerous countries so she can tell the world about the people who live there.

Kira's experiences empower her. Even though she has seen some terrible things, she is still hopeful. Her goal is to find common ground with other people. "When you get beyond politics and superficial cultural differences, people all want the same things: peace, happiness, success for their children, and the best standard of life." Kira is a writer, a traveler, and an adventurer. But above all else, she is a human being. "When someone tells me I can't do something, it just empowers me all the more. People's doubts in my ability only strengthen my resolve. When they say I can't accomplish a challenge, I just eat that up."

D. SUPPORT Underline the answers to the questions below in the reading. Write the question number next to the evidence.

1. How do we know that Kira wanted to travel from a young age?

2. When did she first travel alone?

3. What empowers Kira?

4. Where was she kidnapped?

E. SUMMARIZE Without looking at the reading, tell your partner about Kira's goal, an obstacle, and a solution.

Reading Challenge   35

• Carefully crafted activities help prepare students for college and career success.

• **NEW Reading Challenge** in every unit features a fascinating story about a **National Geographic explorer** to immerse learners in authentic content.

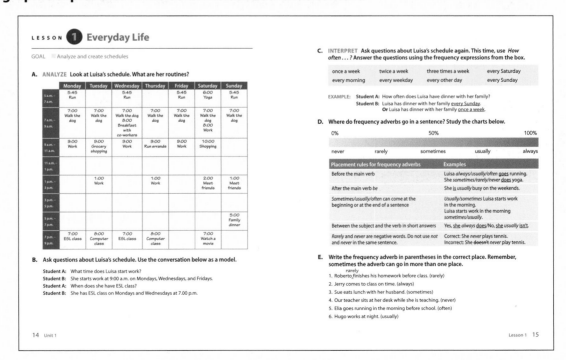

LESSON 1 Everyday Life

GOAL   ■ Analyze and create schedules

A. ANALYZE Look at Luisa's schedule. What are her routines?

	Monday	Tuesday	Wednesday	Thursday	Friday	Saturday	Sunday
5 a.m.–7 a.m.	5:45 Run		5:45 Run		5:45 Run	6:00 Yoga	5:45 Run
7 a.m.–9 a.m.	7:00 Walk the dog	7:00 Walk the dog	7:00 Walk the dog 8:00 Breakfast with co-workers	7:00 Walk the dog	7:00 Walk the dog	7:00 Walk the dog 8:00 Work	7:00 Walk the dog
9 a.m.–11 a.m.	9:00 Work	9:00 Grocery shopping	9:00 Work	9:00 Run errands	9:00 Work	10:00 Shopping	
11 a.m.–1 p.m.							
1 p.m.–3 p.m.		1:00 Work		1:00 Work		2:00 Meet friends	1:00 Meet friends
3 p.m.–5 p.m.							
5 p.m.–7 p.m.							5:00 Family dinner
7 p.m.–9 p.m.	7:00 ESL class	8:00 Computer class	7:00 ESL class	8:00 Computer class	7:00 Watch a movie		

B. Ask questions about Luisa's schedule. Use the conversation below as a model.

Student A: What time does Luisa start work?
Student B: She starts work at 9:00 a.m. on Mondays, Wednesdays, and Fridays.
Student A: When does she have ESL class?
Student B: She has ESL class on Mondays and Wednesdays at 7.00 p.m.

14   Unit 1

C. INTERPRET Ask questions about Luisa's schedule again. This time, use *How often . . . ?* Answer the questions using the frequency expressions from the box.

once a week	twice a week	three times a week	every Saturday
every morning	every weekday	every other day	every Sunday

EXAMPLE: **Student A:** How often does Luisa have dinner with her family?
Student B: Luisa has dinner with her family *every Sunday.*
Or Luisa has dinner with her family *once a week.*

D. Where do frequency adverbs go in a sentence? Study the charts below.

0%		50%		100%
never	rarely	sometimes	usually	always

Placement rules for frequency adverbs	Examples
Before the main verb	Luisa *always/usually/often* goes running. She *sometimes/rarely/never* does yoga.
After the main verb *be*	She *is usually* busy on the weekends.
Sometimes/usually/often can come at the beginning or at the end of a sentence.	*Usually/sometimes* Luisa starts work in the morning. Luisa starts work in the morning *sometimes/usually.*
Between the subject and the verb in short answers	Yes, she *always* does/No, she *usually* isn't.
Rarely and *never* are negative adverbs. Do not use *not* and *never* in the same sentence.	Correct: She *never* plays tennis. Incorrect: She doesn't *never* play tennis.

E. Write the frequency adverb in parentheses in the correct place. Remember, sometimes the adverb can go in more than one place.

1. Roberto finishes his homework before class. (rarely)   *rarely*

2. Jerry comes to class on time. (always)

3. Sue eats lunch with her husband. (sometimes)

4. Our teacher sits at her desk while she is teaching. (never)

5. Elia goes running in the morning before school. (often)

6. Hugo works at night. (usually)

Lesson 1   15

• **EXPANDED Critical Thinking Activities** challenge learners to evaluate, analyze, and synthesize information to prepare them for the workplace and academic life.

- **NEW Video Challenge** showcases **National Geographic footage and explorers**, providing learners with the opportunity to synthesize what they have learned in prior units through the use of authentic content.

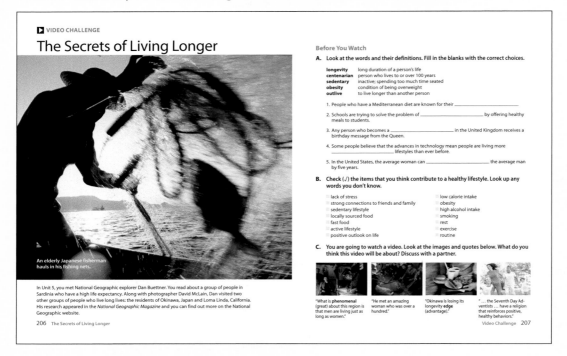

▶ VIDEO CHALLENGE

The Secrets of Living Longer

An elderly Japanese fisherman hauls in his fishing nets.

In Unit 5, you met National Geographic explorer Dan Buettner. You read about a group of people in Sardinia who have a high life expectancy. Along with photographer David McLain, Dan visited two other groups of people who live long lives: the residents of Okinawa, Japan and Loma Linda, California. His research appeared in the *National Geographic Magazine* and you can find out more on the National Geographic website.

206   The Secrets of Living Longer

Before You Watch

A. Look at the words and their definitions. Fill in the blanks with the correct choices.

longevity	long duration of a person's life
centenarian	person who lives to or over 100 years
sedentary	inactive; spending too much time seated
obesity	condition of being overweight
outlive	to live longer than another person

1. People who have a Mediterranean diet are known for their _____

2. Schools are trying to solve the problem of _____ by offering healthy meals to students.

3. Any person who becomes a _____ in the United Kingdom receives a birthday message from the Queen.

4. Some people believe that the advances in technology mean people are living more _____ lifestyles than ever before.

5. In the United States, the average woman can _____ the average man by five years.

B. Check (✓) the items that you think contribute to a healthy lifestyle. Look up any words you don't know.

- lack of stress
- strong connections to friends and family
- sedentary lifestyle
- locally sourced food
- fast food
- active lifestyle
- positive outlook on life
- low calorie intake
- obesity
- high alcohol intake
- smoking
- rest
- exercise
- routine

C. You are going to watch a video. Look at the images and quotes below. What do you think this video will be about? Discuss with a partner.

"What is **phenomenal** (great) about this region is that men are living just as long as women."

"He met an amazing woman who was over a hundred."

"Okinawa is losing its longevity **edge** (advantage)."

" ... the Seventh Day Adventists ... have a religion that reinforces positive, healthy behaviors."

Video Challenge   207

LIFESKILLS ▶ My Schedule is Crazy

Before You Watch

A. Look at the picture and answer the questions.

1. What's wrong with Hector?
2. What do you think Naomi is saying to Hector?

While You Watch

B. ▶ Watch the video and complete the dialog.

Naomi: . . . you wouldn't skip a day of work, either. Treat your studies in the same way, and your grades will (1) __improve__

Hector: That's a great (2) _____ thanks.

Naomi: Well, now you know what you have to do. So go do it! If you get (3) _____, you'll feel more productive. Trust me!

Hector: (4) _____ give it a try. What have I got to lose, right?

Naomi: Good luck. Tell me how it's (5) _____ later on.

Hector: I (6) _____. Talk to you later.

Check Your Understanding

C. Circle the correct word to complete each sentence.

1. There's too much noise and it's difficult for Hector to (communicate/concentrate).

2. Hector says his (schedule/organization) is crazy and he has no time to study.

3. Naomi suggests that Hector (make time/write down) where and when he going to study.

4. A schedule will help Hector to (get organized/spend time with friends).

5. Naomi tells Hector a schedule will make him (productive/smarter).

Lifeskills Video   29

- The **Lifeskills Video** is a dramatic video series integrated into each unit of the student book that helps students learn natural spoken English and apply it to their everyday activities.

Pages shown are from *Stand Out*, Third Edition Level 3

- **NEW Online Workbook** engages students and supports the classroom by providing a wide variety of auto-graded interactive activities, an audio program, video from National Geographic, and pronunciation activities.

- **UPDATED Lesson Planner** includes correlations to **College and Career Readiness Standards (CCRS)**, **CASAS, SCANS** and reference to **EL Civics** competencies to help instructors achieve the required standards.

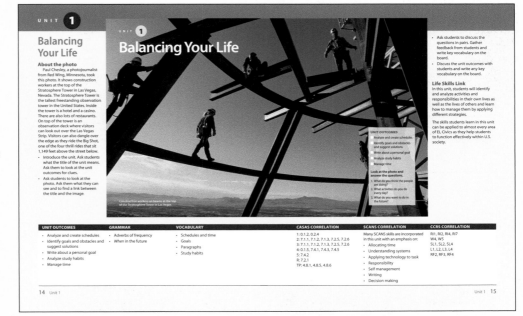

- **Teacher support** *Stand Out* continues to provide a wide variety of user-friendly tools and interactive activities that help teachers prepare students for success while keeping them engaged and motivated.

Stand Out supports teachers and learners

LEARNER COMPONENTS

- Student Book
- Online workbook powered by My**ELT**
- Print workbook

TEACHER COMPONENTS

- Lesson Planner
- Classroom DVD
- Assessment CD-ROM
- Teacher's companion site with Multi-Level Worksheets

Welcome

UNIT OUTCOMES

- Fill out an admission application
- Identify learning strategies
- Write about your goals

LESSON **1** Tell me something about yourself

GOAL ▪ Fill out an admission application

A. Fill out the college admission application below.

CANYON COUNTY COLLEGE
Admission Application

1. Last Name _____   First Name _____   Middle Initial _____

2. Date of Birth (mm/dd/yy) _____ / _____ / _____   Age _____

3. Place of Birth (City, State, or Foreign Country) _____

4. Current Address (Number and Street/ Apt #) _____

City _____   State _____   Zip Code _____

5. (Area Code) Telephone Number (_____) _____

6. Mother's Maiden Name _____

7. Citizen of what country? _____

8. What is the highest level of education you have achieved? _____

9. What is your educational goal? _____

CD 1
TR 1

B. **Read the conversation. Then, listen to the conversation.**

Bita: Hi. My name is Bita. What's your name?

Minh: I'm Minh. Nice to meet you.

Bita: Where are you from, Minh?

Minh: I'm from Vietnam. And you?

Bita: I'm from Iran.

Minh: Interesting. I've never been to Iran. Tell me something about yourself.

Bita: Well, I'm studying English because I want to be an architect in the United States.

Minh: Wow! That's ambitious. Good for you!

Bita: And tell me something about yourself, Minh.

Minh: In my free time, I make jewelry and sell it to help raise money for my grandchildren to go to college.

Bita: That's wonderful! I'd love to see your jewelry sometime.

Minh: I'd be more than happy to show it to you.

C. **DEMONSTRATE** **Talk to three classmates. Find out their first names, where they are from, and one other piece of interesting information about them. Then, introduce your new friends to another group of students.**

First Name	Country	Interesting Information

D. Find the three students you talked to in Exercise C. Ask them about what they wrote on their applications on page 3. Use the questions below to help you get started. What are some other questions you might ask about their applications? Write two more questions.

What is your educational goal?	Where were you born?
What is the highest level of education you have achieved?	What is your mother's maiden name?

1. _____

2. _____

E. Work with a group. Write three questions you want to ask your classmates to help you get to know them.

1. _____

2. _____

3. _____

F. APPLY Interview *other* classmates and write their answers to your group's questions in the chart below. Go back to your group and share the information.

Name	Question 1	Question 2	Question 3
1.			
2.			
3.			
4.			

LESSON **2** Learning strategies

GOAL ■ Identify learning strategies

A. **How do you learn English? Make a list.**

1. _Go to school._

2. _____

3. _____

4. _____

5. _____

6. _____

B. **Learning a new language takes place inside and outside the classroom. Below is a list of strategies you can use to learn a new language. Read them with your teacher.**

Learning Strategies

Learn grammar rules.

Listen to the radio in English.

Read English books, magazines, and newspapers.

Talk to native speakers.

Watch TV in English.

Write in English.

C. **Think of other learning strategies and add them to the list above.**

D. EVALUATE Answer the questions about your personal studying strategies.

1. Where do you usually study? _____

_____

2. What strategies do you use inside the classroom? _____

_____

3. What strategies do you use outside the classroom? _____

_____

4. Write two strategies that you don't use now, but that you would like to use in the future. _____

_____

_____

5. What do you think is the best strategy for learning English? _____

_____

E. Interview other students in your class using the questions in Exercise D. Write their answers below.

	Student 1	Student 2	Student 3
Study Locations			
Classroom Strategies			
Outside Strategies			
New Strategies to Use			
Best Strategies			

F. Look at the bar graph and answer the questions.

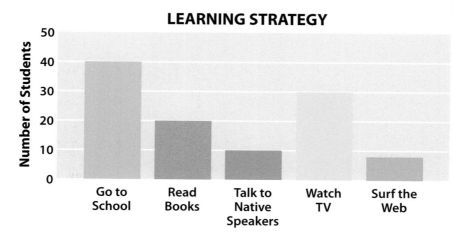

How many students . . .

go to school?   _____

read books?   _____

talk to native speakers? _____

watch TV?   _____

surf the Web?   _____

G. **CONSTRUCT** Create a bar graph. With a group, decide on six effective learning strategies. Take a class poll to see how many people use these learning strategies.

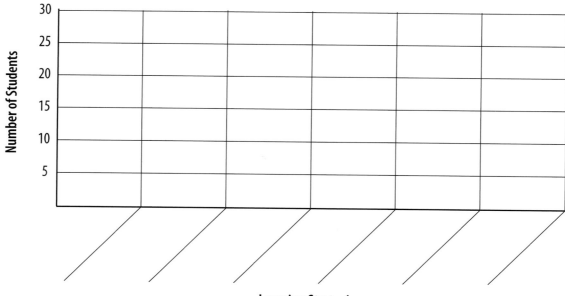

LESSON ③ What are your goals?

GOAL ▪ Write about your goals

A. In this book, you will be learning many new strategies to help you learn and remember vocabulary. The first strategy involves word families. What do you think a word family is? Look at the example below.

Noun	Verb	Adjective	Adverb
creation	create	creative	creatively

B. Read the paragraph. There are five words that belong to the same word family. Find and underline them.

> My goal for the year is to get organized. To learn a new language, you need to study a lot of vocabulary. Good organization requires writing down the new words you learn and finding out their meanings. You should organize the words in a notebook so you can easily find them. Once you learn how to keep a well-organized vocabulary list, you can say, "I have good organizational skills!"

C. Complete the chart with word families. You may need to use a dictionary or ask another student for help.

Noun	Verb	Adjective	Adverb
		educational	
success			
	decide		
		achievable	

D. VISUALIZE The student who wrote the paragraph in Exercise B has a goal—to get organized. What are your goals for the year? List them below.

My Goals

E. Takuji has had three goals since he came to the United States. Read his paragraph. What are his three goals?

My Goals

Ever since I came to the United States, I have had three goals. First, I want to improve my English by going to school every day and studying at night. Then, once my English is better, I will look for a job that pays more money. Finally, when I have saved up enough money, I will buy a new house for my family. These are the three goals that I made when I first came to the United States.

F. What is a paragraph? Discuss the words in italics with your teacher.

A paragraph is a group of sentences (usually 5–7 sentences) about the *same topic*. A *topic sentence* is usually the first sentence and it introduces your topic or *main idea*. *Support sentences* are the sentences that follow your topic sentence. They give *details* about your topic. A *conclusion sentence* is the last sentence of your paragraph and it summarizes what you have written.

PARAGRAPH
Topic sentence
Support sentences (4–5 sentences)
Conclusion sentence

G. Look back at Takuji's paragraph. Can you find each of the three sentence types discussed in Exercise F?

H. COMPOSE What are your goals? Write a paragraph about your goals on a piece of paper. Make sure your first sentence is a topic sentence. Follow your topic sentence with support sentences and then, finish your paragraph with a conclusion sentence.

I. ANALYZE Look at the first draft of Takuji's paragraph. There are eight errors. The first one has been done for you. Can you find and correct the rest?

My Goals

Ever since I came to the United States, I have had three goal. First
I need to improve my English by going at school every day and studying
at night. Once my English are better, I will look for a job that pays more
money. Finally, when I have saved up enough money. I will buy a house new
for my family. This are the three goals that I made when I first come to
the united States.

J. Write each of the errors from the paragraph in the chart below. Then, write the correct form and identify the type of error. Use choices from the box.

punctuation	capitalization	subject/verb agreement	verb tense
spelling	singular/plural	word choice	word order

Error	Correction	Type of Error
goal	goals	singular/plural
Come	Came	Spelling
a house New	a New House	Word Order
at	to	Verb tense
	Then	
.	,	Punctuation

K. EVALUATE Now, exchange the paragraph you wrote in Exercise H with a partner. Check your partner's work for errors using the error types listed in Exercise J.

Balancing Your Life

The cyclist comes to a fork in the road. He needs to make a decision about which road to take. Balancing your life also requires choices.

UNIT OUTCOMES

- ☐ Compare past and present
- ☐ Determine goals
- ☐ Identify obstacles and give advice
- ☐ Write about an important person
- ☐ Identify and apply time-management skills

Look at the photo and answer the questions.

1. What to do you see in the picture?
2. Why does the cyclist have to make a choice?
3. What type of choices do you make in your life?

LESSON 1 Where did you use to study?

GOAL ▪ Compare past and present

🎧 **A.** Bita and Minh are new students at Bellingham Adult School. Listen to their
CD 1 conversation about their first day of class.
TR 2

B. **PREDICT** With a partner, answer the questions about Bita and Minh. You may have
to guess some of the answers.

Minh

Bita

1. How old are they?

2. What do they do?

3. Where are they from?

4. Why are they studying English?

🎧 **C.** Bita and Minh both talk about things they did in the past and things they do now.
CD 1 Listen again and complete the chart.
TR 3

	Past	Now
Bita	went to another school in the daytime	
Minh		

D. **Study the chart with your classmates and teacher.**

Used to	
Example	**Rule**
Minh *used to* go to school during the day. Bita *used to* be an architect in Iran.	**Affirmative:** *used to* + base verb
Bita *did not use to* go to school at night. Minh *didn't use to* take care of his grandchildren.	**Negative:** *did + not (didn't) + use to* + base verb **Incorrect:** ~~I didn't used to go to school.~~
Did Minh *use to* work? *Did* Bita *use to* study English?	**Yes/No Question:** *did* + subject + *use to* + base verb **Incorrect:** ~~Did Bita used to live in Iran?~~
Where *did* Minh *use to* work? What *did* Bita *use to* study?	**Wh- Question:** *wh-* word + *did* + subject + *use to* + base verb
Used to + base verb expresses a past habit or state that is now different.	

E. **Complete the sentences with the correct form of *used to* and the verb in parentheses.**

1. Kaitlin ___used to live___ (live) with her family, but now she ___lives___ (live) alone.

2. Armando ___Used to go___ (go) to school in the daytime, but now he ___go___ (go) in the evening.

3. Where did Su ___Used to teach___ (teach)?

4. Heidi ___is___ (be) an administrative assistant now, but she ___Used to be___ (be) an architect in Sweden.

5. He ___go___ (go) to school and ___help___ (help) his children now, but he ___Used to assemble___ (assemble) computers.

6. Elisa ___Used to live___ (live) near her family, but now she ___lives___ (live) far away.

7. Did the two brothers ___Used to study___ (study) together?

8. Andres ___Use to work___ (not work) at night. [*Not*]

9. Iva ___Not Use to teach___ (not teach) kindergarten.

F. Look back at the things that you wrote about Bita and Minh in Exercise C. With a partner, make sentences about what Bita and Minh *used* to do and what they do now.

1. Bita used to go to another school in the daytime, but now she goes to school in the evening.

2. _____

3. _____

4. _____

G. Write three *Wh-* questions using *used* to. Then, ask a partner your questions.

1. Where did you use to work?

2. ~~Where~~ What did you use to Study?

3. Where you used to leave?

4. Which did Use to level in ~~English~~ English?

H. Look at the pictures. With a partner, make sentences comparing the past and the present.

Subject / Verb	Past	Present
1. Suzanne / play		
2. Eli and Rosa / live		

I. **COMPARE** Write two sentences comparing your past and present habits.

1. _____

2. _____

LESSON ② Reaching your goals

GOAL ■ Determine goals

A. **INFER** Read the paragraph about Bita's goals. Use the context (surrounding words) to work out the meanings of the words in *italics*. Do the first one with your teacher.

My name is Bita and I'm from Iran. I've been in the United States for six years. In my country, I was an *architect* and I designed schools and hospitals, but in the United States, I don't have the right *qualifications* to be an architect. I have a plan. I'm going to learn English, go to school for architecture, and become an architect in the U.S. Here is my dream: In nine years, I will be an architect working in a *firm* with three other partners. We will design and build homes in *suburban* neighborhoods. I will live in a nice home that I designed. How does that sound to you?

B. **INFER** Read the paragraph about Minh. Use the context to work out the meanings of the words in *italics*.

I'm Minh and I've been in the United States since 1975. I came here as a *refugee* from Vietnam. I used to work for a computer company, but now I'm *retired*. I help take care of my grandchildren while their parents are working, but I also do something else on the side. I make jewelry to sell to local jewelers. My father was a jeweler in Vietnam, and he taught me his art. My goal is to help send my grandchildren to college, so I save every penny I make from the jewelry. This is my dream: In five years, my oldest grandchild will teach elementary school in the community where she lives, and she will *raise* her own family. My other grandchild will study medicine at one of the best schools in the country because he wants to be a *surgeon*. I hope that all of their dreams come true.

C. Answer the questions with a partner.

1. What are Bita's and Minh's goals?

2. What are they doing to make their goals a reality?

3. What are their dreams?

D. **CLASSIFY** Make a list of three school goals and three personal goals. Compare your goals with a partner. Discuss your ideas with your teacher.

E. What are your future goals? Write them on a piece of paper.

F. Listen to the conversation that Bita is having with her friend, Yoshiko. Fill in Bita's goal chart with the missing steps and dates.

Goal: To become an architect and a partner in a firm	
Steps	**Completion Dates**
Step 1: I will study English.	Spring 2016
Step 2:	Fall 2016
Step 3:	
Step 4: I will become an intern.	Summer 2019
Step 5:	Winter 2020
Step 6: I will become a partner in a firm.	2021

G. **PREDICT** Turn back to page 17 and look at the paragraph about Minh. With a partner, create a goal chart for Minh based on the steps you think it will take Minh to achieve his goal.

Goal: For my granddaughter to be a teacher and my grandson to be a surgeon	
Steps	**Completion Dates**
Step 1:	
Step 2:	
Step 3:	
Step 4:	
Step 5: My granddaughter will be a teacher, and my grandson will be a surgeon.	

H. Share your ideas with another pair of students.

I. Look back at the goals you wrote in Exercise E. Choose the most important goal and write it below.

My goal: _____

By what year do you want to achieve your goal?

_____

J. **PLAN** Look at the goal chart below. Write your goal at the top. Write your goal again next to "Step 6," and write the date you will complete this goal. Now, fill in the chart with the steps it will take to reach this goal. Estimate your completion dates.

Goal: _____	
Steps	**Completion Dates**
Step 1:	
Step 2:	
Step 3:	
Step 4:	
Step 5:	
Step 6:	

K. Now, talk to a partner about your goal and the steps that you will take to achieve it.

EXAMPLE: In the fall of 2016, I will take classes at a community college.

Future Tense Using *Will*	
Example	**Rule**
In the spring of 2015, I *will ask* my boss for a raise. In the summer, I *will look* for a job. In the winter, she *will volunteer* at the school.	Future tense = *will* + base verb
In spoken English, people often use contractions: *I will* = *I'll*.	

LESSON ❸ What should I do?

GOAL ▪ Identify obstacles and give advice

A. Sometimes we have problems achieving our goals. These problems are called *obstacles*. In order to overcome these obstacles, it can be a good idea to brainstorm different possible solutions. Look at the diagram below.

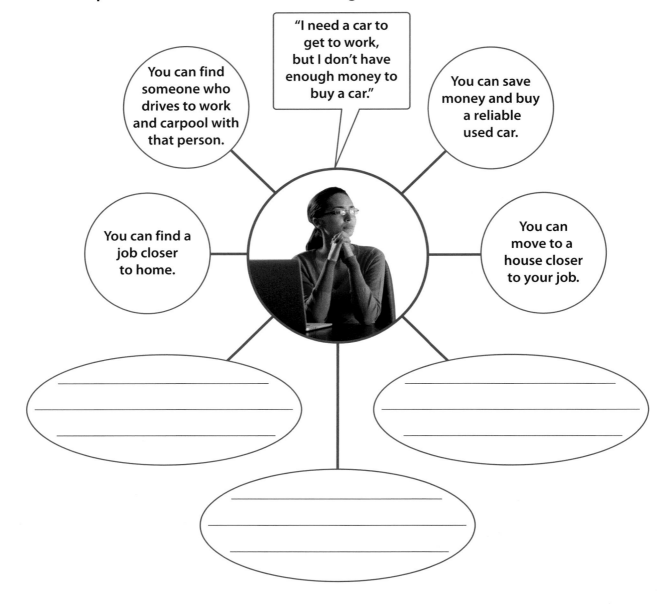

"I need a car to get to work, but I don't have enough money to buy a car."

You can find someone who drives to work and carpool with that person.

You can save money and buy a reliable used car.

You can find a job closer to home.

You can move to a house closer to your job.

B. **GENERATE** Can you think of any other solutions? Add them to the blank circles in the cluster diagram above.

C. Listen to each person talk to his or her friends about their problems. After you listen to each conversation, write the problem and two pieces of advice that the person receives.

Miyuki	Problem	Advice #1	Advice #2
(photo)	down Angry Studen week Try go Teacher Better		
Ron *(photo)*	Dogs herby Friendly Any dogs other Aparment		
Patty *(photo)*	Money Operacion expence Job		

D. Read the ways of giving and responding to advice in the chart below.

Problem	Advice
Magda wants to go back to school, but she has two children that she has to take care of. One of them is a toddler who isn't in school yet.	*Why don't you* ask your mother to take care of him? *How about* going to school in the evening? *You should* take some courses at home on the Internet. *You could* find a school with a daycare facility.

Response to Advice (Positive)	Response to Advice (Negative)
That's a great idea!	I don't think I can do that because . . .
Why didn't I think of that?	That doesn't sound possible because . . .
That's what I'll do.	That won't work because . . .

E. SUPPOSE Read the situations and come up with two possible solutions for each. Use *could* when writing your solutions.

1. Magda wants to go back to school, but she has two children that she has to take care of. One of her children is a toddler who isn't in school yet.

   Solution: *She could ask a family member to take care of her toddler so she can go to school*

   during the day.

2. Frank wants to open a restaurant in his neighborhood. He can get a loan to buy the property, but he won't have enough money to pay his employees until the restaurant starts making money.

   Solution 1: _____

   _____

   Solution 2: _____

   _____

3. Sergei works for a computer software company and wants to be promoted to project manager. The problem is that he needs to get more training before he can move up, but he doesn't have time to do training during the day.

   Solution 1: _____

   _____

   Solution 2: _____

   _____

F. Work with a partner. Imagine that one of you has one of the problems in Exercise E. Make a new conversation like the one below. Use different ways of giving and responding to advice.

Student A: I want to go back to school, but I have a young child to take care of.
Student B: Why don't you ask your mother to take care of him?
Student A: That won't work because she lives too far away.
Student B: Then, how about taking some courses on the Internet?
Student A: That's a good idea!

G. CREATE Look back at Exercise J on page 19. Think of an obstacle that might get in your way of achieving this goal. Make a cluster diagram like the one on page 20 and brainstorm different solutions with a partner.

LESSON ④ What is most important to me?

GOAL ▦ Write about an important person

A. Look at the photos and listen to Eliana talk about why they are important to her. Then, read the paragraphs.

This is a picture of the house where I grew up in Argentina. It's very important to me because it holds a lot of memories. This is the garden where I played with my brothers and sisters, and the veranda where I often sat with my parents in the evenings, listening to their stories and watching the stars and dreaming about my future.

This is the person who influenced me the most when I was young. She was my teacher in the first grade and we stayed friends until I left home. She was always so calm and gave me good advice. She was the kind of person who is able to give you another perspective on a problem and make you feel hopeful, no matter how troubled you are.

This is my daily journal. I use it to write about my feelings and hopes. It helps me understand them better. Sometimes I just write about things which happened to me during the day. My journal is something which helps me focus on the important things in my life.

B. Read the paragraphs again and underline the words *who, which,* and *where.* Write the sentences you found for each. When do we use these words? Circle the correct answers below.

1. We use (*which /* ⟨*where*⟩ */ who*) for places.

_____

2. We use (*which / where /* ⟨*who*⟩) for people.

_____

3. We use ⟨*which*⟩ */ where / who*) for things.

_____

C. Study the chart with your teacher.

Adjective Clauses		
Main clause (Subject clause)	**Relative pronoun**	**Adjective clause**
This is the place	where	I grew up.
She is the person	who (that)	influenced me most.
A journal is something	which (that)	can help you focus on important things.
Main clause (Object clause)	**Relative pronoun**	**Adjective clause**
This is the woman	who (whom)	I met yesterday.
Here is the book	which (that)	you gave me this morning.
Adjectival clauses describe a preceding noun. They can describe a subject noun or an object noun. If the noun is an object, you can leave out the relative pronoun.		

D. Combine the sentences using adjective clauses. In which sentence can you leave out the relative pronoun?

1. This is the house. I grew up there.

   This is the house where I grew up.

2. That is the city. I was born there.

   That is the city Where I borned

3. I have a friend. She helps me when I am sick.

   I have a friend who helps me when I'm siak

4. We have some neighbors. They are very friendly.

   We have some neighbors who are very friendly

5. This is the gold ring. My mother bought it for me.

   This is the gold ring that My mother bought it for me.

E. Look at the pictures with a partner and make sentences about them using adjective clauses.

F. Bita wrote a paragraph about her brother. Read the paragraph. With a partner, discuss the questions that follow.

Someone Who Has Influenced Me

The person who has influenced me most in my life is my brother, Karim. I admire my brother for three reasons. First, he has patience and determination. Second, he does a fantastic job helping the community. Third, he is the type of person who always has time for his friends and family, no matter how busy he is. He has had a very positive influence on my life.

1. What type of person is Bita's brother?

2. Why does Bita admire him?

3. How has he influenced Bita?

G. Now, it's your turn to write about a person who has influenced you. Complete these pre-writing activities before you begin.

➤ **Brainstorm** (Think about your ideas before you write.)

Who has influenced you most in your life? _____ My Mother _____

Why is this person so important to you? List three reasons.

1. _____ She always say me " you can do it everything" _____
2. _____ She is my inpiration for doing Better person _____
3. _____ She is the person who can talk anything else _____

➤ **Introduce** (Tell your readers what you are writing about.) Write your topic sentence.

_____

➤ **Conclude** (Remind your reader of the main idea, but don't restate your topic sentence.) Write your conclusion sentence.

_____

H. COMPOSE Now, write a paragraph about an important person in your life. Start with your topic sentence. Put your reasons (support sentences) in the middle of your paragraph and finish with your conclusion sentence.

LESSON **5** Time management

A. **EVALUATE** Are you an organized person? Do you . . .

- ☒ try to do everything, but run out of time?
- ☒ always plan everything far in advance?
- ☐ dislike planning things too far ahead?
- ☒ tend to leave things to the last minute?
- ☒ get upset by last-minute changes to your schedule?
- ☒ only plan for important tasks like exams and job interviews?

Important	Very Important	URGENT!

B. Work with a partner to list time-management strategies that you know.

Time-Management Strategies

1. keep a schedule

C. Talk to other pairs in your class. What are some strategies they came up with that are not on your list? Write them below.

More Time-Management Strategies

Nephew
Neice

Aunt

D. ANALYZE Read the paragraphs about time management. Write the number of the corresponding paragraph next to each topic below.

_____ How can I get everything done?

_____ Why is good health important to time management?

_____ How can I be organized?

_____ How can I manage my time? Why is it important?

_____ How can I get important tasks done first?

Time-Management Strategies

(1) Finding enough time to study is very important for all students. There are a number of time-management strategies that can help you to manage your time wisely. You can use them to *accomplish* the goals you have set for yourself without *sacrificing* the time you spend with your family and friends.

(2) One of the best ways to stay organized is to keep a schedule. First, write down everything you need to do in a week. This includes work, study, taking care of children, shopping, and other tasks. Next, *allocate* a time slot to complete each of these tasks. Be *realistic* about the time you will need for each task. Mark these *deadlines* on your schedule. Finally, check off each task when you have completed it.

(3) It is a good idea to *prioritize* your tasks in order of importance. First, make a "To Do" list of all your tasks. Second, divide your list into three groups: A, B, and C. The A list is for tasks you need to do today. The B list is for tasks you need to do tomorrow. The C list is for tasks you need to do sometime this week. Dividing your list will help you get your most important tasks done first. You can also list tasks according to urgency: tasks you have to do, tasks you should do, and tasks you'd like to do if you have time.

(4) Another time-management strategy is to combine two or more tasks and do them *simultaneously*. You can listen to audio study tapes while you are driving, for example. Or, you can review verb tenses while you are eating lunch.

(5) Lastly, remember that good health is also important to managing your time effectively. If you are burned out or overtired, you cannot do your best. First, you need to allow time for rest and exercise. Also, you need to have time to spend with family, friends, and people who are important to you.

In conclusion, don't get upset if you cannot accomplish all your goals. Be positive about your *achievements* and reward yourself for goals that you have accomplished.

E. **INFER** Find the following words in the time-management reading and use the context to work out their meanings.

accomplish	sacrificing	allocate	realistic
deadlines	prioritize	simultaneously	achievements

F. Use the diagram below to record the main points of the reading.

Time-Management Strategies	Keep a schedule.	Write down everything you need to do in a week.
		Allocate a time slot to complete each task.
		Check off each task when completed.
	Combine two or more tasks.	

G. Think about what you learned today and complete the chart.

My Time-Management Strategies	
Strategies I Use Now	**New Strategies I Will Start Using**

LIFESKILLS ▶ I need to get organized

Before You Watch

A. Look at the picture. Complete each sentence.

1. Naomi is talking to Hector and Mateo about _____.

2. She is making a _____ of tips.

3. Naomi is _____.

While You Watch

B. ▶ Watch the video. Complete the dialog.

Mateo: Well, how did you learn to get (1) ___organized___?

Naomi: Here is your new best friend. I'm going to teach you some time-management skills.

The first one: (2) _____ everything down. Now, write your goals.

Naomi: "Goal setting": You need to make a chart with all your goals and things to do.

"Prioritization": You (3) _____ know what things need to get done first.

Mateo: That's a great idea! I (4) _____ I had thought of that.

Naomi: "Managing interruptions," "Avoiding (5) _____," "Scheduling."

Check Your Understanding

C. Read the statements. Write T for *True* and F for *False*.

1. Hector has a problem with time management.   __F__

2. Hector knows which tasks he has to do first, next, and last.   _____

3. Naomi gives Hector advice about writing papers.   _____

4. Mateo helps Hector with his paper.   _____

5. Naomi tells Hector to write everything down.   _____

Review

Learner Log

I can compare the past and present.   I can create a goal chart.

☐ Yes   ☐ No   ☐ Maybe   ☐ Yes   ☐ No   ☐ Maybe

A. **Make sentences to contrast past and present habits.**

1. Past: I ate meat.   Present: I don't eat meat now.

    I used to eat meat, but now I don't.

2. Past: Paolo didn't have a computer.   Present: He has a computer now.

    Pablo ^{didn't} use to have a Computer, but now he ~~has~~ does

3. Past: Maria swam every day.   Present: She doesn't swim now.

    Maria used to swim every day, but now she doesn't swim

4. Past: My children didn't like vegetables.   Present: They like vegetables now.

    My children use to like vegetables, but now they like

5. Past: I didn't study full-time.   Present: Now, I study full-time.

    I use to study full-time, but now I study full-time) or
                       but now I do

B. **Write four questions that you can ask your partner using the correct form of *used to*. Leave the answer lines blank for now.**

1. *Where did you use to live?*

    Answer: _____

2. What did you use to do in the evenings?

    Answer: _____

3. Which did you use to ^{favorit} food ~~ba~~ in your country?

    Answer: _____

4. _____

    Answer: _____

5. _____

    Answer: _____

Now, ask your partner the questions and write down his or her answers.

Learner Log

I can identify obstacles and give advice.   I can write about an important person.
☐ Yes ☐ No ☐ Maybe   ☐ Yes ☐ No ☐ Maybe

C. Ask a partner about one of his or her goals and complete a goal chart with the information he or she gives you.

Goal: _____	
Steps	**Completion Dates**
Step 1:	
Step 2:	
Step 3:	
Step 4:	

D. Dave wants to study at college, but he needs to work full-time while he is going to school in order to pay for his education and support his family. Dave asks his friend, Camille, for advice. With a partner, create a conversation between the two friends. Make sure Camille suggests two or three different solutions to Dave's problem. Use expressions from this unit for giving and responding to advice.

Dave: _____

Camille: _____

Dave: _____

Camille: _____

Dave: _____

Camille: _____

Dave: _____

E. Combine the sentences using adjective clauses.

1. Esra has many brothers and sisters. They live in Argentina.

_____

2. This is a good grammar book. It can help you improve your writing.

_____

3. I am trying to find a school. I can study computers.

_____

4. E-mail is a type of communication. We use it at home and at work.

_____

F. **Read the list of statements below. Write *TM* next to the ones that are time-management strategies.**

_____ Become an architect.

_____ Buy new clothes.

_TM_ Check off your tasks when you have finished them.

_TM_ Combine two tasks.

_TM_ Prioritize your tasks.

_____ Send your children to college.

_TM_ Set realistic deadlines.

_____ Write about your teacher.

_____ Stay healthy.

_____ Give advice.

_____ Make jewelry.

G. **Use the words from the box to complete the sentences.**

deadline	prioritize	simultaneously	raising	refugee	retired

1. Someone who stops work because they are old is ___retired___ .

2. Someone who escapes from a country because of danger is a ___refugee___ .

3. If you have young children, you are ___raising___ a family.

4. If you are doing things at the same time, you are doing them ___simultaneously___ .

5. If you have to complete a task by a certain time, that is your ___deadline___ .

6. When you put things in order of importance, you ___prioritize___ them.

H. **Vocabulary cards help you practice new words and phrases. Choose five new words you learned and make vocabulary cards.**

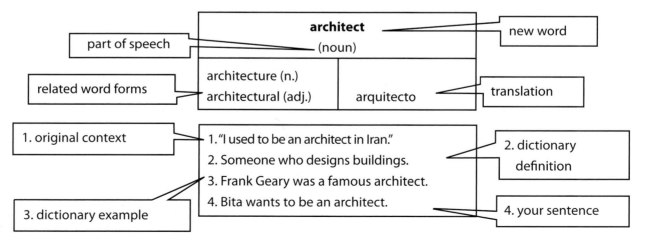

part of speech	**architect**	new word
	(noun)	

| related word forms | architecture (n.) architectural (adj.) | arquitecto | translation |

1. original context	1. "I used to be an architect in Iran."	2. dictionary definition
	2. Someone who designs buildings.	
3. dictionary example	3. Frank Geary was a famous architect.	
	4. Bita wants to be an architect.	4. your sentence

✓ **Create a goal chart**

With a team, you will create a goal chart for goals you want to accomplish in this class.

1. **COLLABORATE** Form a team with four or five students. Choose positions for each member of your team:

Position	Job description	Student name
Student 1: **Team Leader**	Check that everyone speaks English. Check that everyone participates.	
Student 2: **Writer**	Take notes.	
Student 3: **Director**	Design the goal chart.	
Students 4/5: **Spokespeople**	Prepare team for presentation.	
Students 4/5: **Assistant**	Help team members with their jobs.	

2. Decide on one goal that your team would like to accomplish by the end of this class. Make it specific. ("Learn English" is not a very specific goal, but "improve our reading skills" and "learn more vocabulary" are.)

3. Write down the steps it will take to reach this goal. Write down a completion date for each step.

4. Write down two obstacles that might get in the way of achieving your goal and possible solutions for each one.

5. Make a list of three time-management techniques that will help you reach your goal.

6. Design a goal chart that includes all of the information from Steps 2–5.

7. Present your chart to the class.

EXPLORER KAKENYA NTAIYA

Empowering Girls

"I want school not only to empower Kenya's girls, but also their mothers, fathers, and entire villages."
—Kakenya Ntaiya

A. Read about Kakenya.

Name: Kakenya Ntaiya

Goal: to become a teacher

Obstacles: 1. extreme poverty so no money for school

2. busy plowing the fields and helping to care for my younger siblings

3. education not important for girls

B. COMPOSE **Write a paragraph about Kakenya using the prompts below.**

(Topic Sentence: Kakenya's Goal) _____

_____. But, I have three main obstacles.

First, _____. Second, _____

_____. (Conclusion Sentence) And finally,

_____.

C.   PREDICT   Discuss with your classmates. What could be some possible solutions to Kakenya's obstacles?

D.   Read about Kakenya.

Kakenya is changing education for girls in her country of Kenya. She is the oldest of eight children and the odds were against her. She grew up in a grass and mud hut that her family shared with the goats and sheep. Her family was poor and she had to work to support them and help take care of her siblings. Only 11% of the girls from her country continue on past elementary school, but Kakenya was determined to finish school and become a teacher. She convinced her father to let her go to high school. When her father became sick and their family had no money, she persuaded the village leader to help her and he convinced the community to financially support her education. Not only did she go to college and get her BA in International Studies and Political Science, but she went on to get her PhD in Education from the University of Pittsburgh. Kakeyna was the first girl from her village to go to college.

Kakenya became so much more than a teacher. She went back to Kenya and opened The Kakenya Center for Excellence, an academy for girls. The classes are very small and she hopes to accept 30 new girls every year. In addition to studying academic subjects, the girls learn to become leaders. "After just a few months here, they become completely different people," Ntaiya observes. "In a girls-only environment they lead, make decisions, speak up, and gain confidence. They're smart and thriving. They just needed a chance." Kakenya hopes that other academies like hers will be started in other remote areas of her country. "I'm helping girls who cannot speak for themselves. Why should they go through the hardships I endured? They'll be stepping on my shoulders to move up the ladder—they're not going to start on the bottom."

E.   Answer the following questions with a partner.

1. How did Kakenya overcome her obstacles?

2. Name three successful things that she has done.

3. If you were going to open a school, what would it be like? Where would it be? What would you teach?

F.   Kakenya said, "Be the first. People will follow you." What do you think she means by this?

_____

_____

_____

Personal Finance

A jazz musician's birthday party in the
French Quarter of New Orleans, Louisiana

UNIT OUTCOMES

☐ Calculate expenses

☐ Identify ways to be a smart consumer

☐ Interpret credit card and loan information

☐ Analyze advertising techniques

☐ Write a business letter

Look at the photo and answer the questions.

1. What do you see in the picture?

2. What are the people doing?

3. What will the man do with the money?

LESSON **1** Money in, money out

GOAL ■ Calculate expenses

A. Think about your personal finances. What do you spend money on every month? Make a list.

_____   _____
_____   _____
_____   _____
_____   _____
_____   _____
_____   _____
_____   _____

🎧 **B.** Listen to Sara and Todd Mason talk about their finances. Fill in the missing numbers.
CD 1
TR 7

Monthly Expenses	
Auto	$550
Cable/Phone/Internet	
Clothing	
Entertainment	
Food	
Medical	
Rent	$1,500
School Supplies	
Utilities (gas, electricity, water)	

C. **COMPARE** Look at your expenses and the Masons' expenses. What are the similarities? What are the differences?

D. Look at the chart. The *Budgeted Amount* column is how much the Masons think they will spend. Look at the numbers you wrote in Exercise B. Complete the column.

Monthly Expenses	Budgeted Amount	Actual Amount	Difference
Auto	$550	$445.50	104.50
Cable/Phone/Internet	$190	235.72	−45.72
Clothing	$200	102.14	97.86
Entertainment	$150	132.96	17.04
Food	$600	659.81	−59.81
Medical	$50	45.28	4.72
Rent	$1,500	$1,500	$0
School Supplies	$60	36	30
Utilities	$160	208.12	48.12
TOTAL			

🎧 **E.** Listen to Sara and Todd talk about what they actually spent. Complete the *Actual Amount* column.

CD 1
TR 8

F. CALCULATE Look at the "TOTAL" row. This is the total budgeted amount and the total amount the Masons actually spent. Practice adding the numbers to get the totals. Complete the totals on your own.

1.
$1,500.00
+$550.00
$2,050.00

2.
$1,300.00
+$475.60

3.
$875.42
$165.00
+$45.70

4.
$900.00
$32.75
$450.00
+$76.22

5.
$234.56
$987.23
$39.00
+$75.11

G. CALCULATE Complete the totals for the *Budgeted Amount* and the *Actual Amount* columns in Exercise D.

H. CALCULATE Look at the *Difference* column in Exercise D. This is the difference between the *Budgeted Amount* and the *Actual Amount*. Look at the first example and then complete the other differences on your own. Remember that when doing subtraction, the larger number must be on top.

1.
$550.00
−$445.50
$104.50

2.
$1,300.00
−$475.60

3.
$875.42
−$165.00

4.
$450.00
−$76.22

5.
$987.23
−$75.11

I. Sometimes the Masons budgeted less than they spent. In this case, you still do the subtraction with the larger number on top, but the end result is a negative number. The items below are for practice. Look at the first example and then complete the other differences on your own.

They budgeted:	$160.00	$85.00	$200.00
They spent:	$208.12	$100.10	$213.45

1.
$208.12
−$160.00
$48.12

2.
$100.10
−$85.00

3.
$213.45
−$200.00

J. Complete the differences between the *Budgeted Amount* and the *Actual Amount*. Write the answers in the chart in Exercise D.

K. CREATE Make a budget of your own. List each expense with a budgeted amount. Then, at the end of the month list the actual amount and find the difference.

LESSON 2 Savvy shopper

GOAL ■ Identify ways to be a smart consumer

A. PREDICT The Masons want to buy a good-quality couch that will last a long time. What do you think they will do before buying the couch? Discuss your ideas with your classmates.

B. Sara did some research on the Internet. Read the web page below to see what information she found.

http://www.smartconsumer.com

How to Be a Smart Consumer
Buying an expensive item can be a bit scary.
To get the most for your money, try the following tips.

Budget. Plan carefully before you shop. Determine a budget and stick to it.

Shop around. Shop around for quality and price, as well as for credit terms and service. Many stores now offer the option to finance. If you take this route, find out what the seller's credit terms are. Remember, a "sale" price isn't always the "best" price.

Read sale ads carefully. Some may say "quantities limited," "no rain checks," or "not available at all stores." Also, some ads contain misleading information.

Look for price-matching policies. Some merchants will match, or even beat, their competitors' prices. Read the merchant's pricing policy carefully. It may not apply to all items.

Go online. Check out Internet sites that compare prices for items offered online. Some sites also may compare prices offered at stores in your area. If you decide to buy online, keep shipping costs and delivery time in mind.

Carefully consider bargain offers that are based on purchases of additional merchandise. For example, "Buy one, get one free" or "Free gift with purchase": If you don't really want or need the item, it's not a deal.

Ask about refund and return policies for sale items. Merchants may have different refund and return policies for sale items, especially clearance merchandise.

Ask about warranties. Most items have some sort of guarantee. Also, some stores will extend the warranty or offer an extended warranty for you to purchase. Decide if this is necessary based on the product you are buying.

C. Based on the reading in Exercise B, list six things you should do before you make an expensive purchase.

1. _____

2. _____

3. _____

4. _____

5. _____

6. _____

D. **SUPPOSE** Sometimes being a smart consumer means not buying something even when you want it. If you had all the money in the world, what two items would you buy?

1. _____   2. _____

Now, look at these examples:

1. If I were rich, I would buy a new car. (I'm not really rich, so I can't buy a new car.)

2. If they had a million dollars, they would move to Beverly Hills. (They don't have a million dollars, so they can't move to Beverly Hills.)

These statements are called *contrary-to-fact conditionals*. They express a condition and a result that are not true at this point in time.

E. Study the chart with your teacher.

Contrary-to-Fact Conditionals	
Condition (*if* + past tense verb)	**Result (*would* + base verb)**
If she *got* a raise,	she *would buy* a new house.
If they *didn't spend* so much money on rent,	they *would have* more money for entertainment.
If I *were* a millionaire,	I *would give* all my money to charity.
If John *weren't* so busy at work,	he *would spend* more time with his children.

- *Contrary-to-fact* (or *unreal*) *conditional statements* are sentences that are not true.
- The *if*-clause can come in the first or second part of the sentence. Notice how commas are used in the examples. (If you reverse the order of the condition and result clauses, omit the comma.)
- In written English, use *were* (instead of *was*) for *if*-clauses with first- and third-person singular forms of *be*.
- In spoken English, people often use contractions: I would = *I'd*; she would = *she'd*, etc.

F. Complete the sentences with the correct form of the verbs in parentheses.

1. If Bita _____ (be) an architect in the United States, she

   _____ (design) beautiful homes.

2. Van's parents _____ (purchase) a new computer if they

   _____ (have) some extra money.

3. If my husband _____ (be) rich, he _____ (buy)
   me an expensive diamond ring.

4. George _____ (save) more money if he _____
   (not spend) so much on eating out.

5. You _____ (not be) so tired if you _____ (have)
   more time to relax.

G. Study the chart with your teacher.

Contrary-to-Fact Questions	
Wh– Question	*Yes/No* Question
What + would + subject + base verb + *if* + subject + past tense	*Would* + subject + base verb + *if* + subject + past tense
What would you do *if* you won the lottery?	*Would* you give up your job *if* you won the lottery?

H. Work in groups. Practice the conversation. Make new conversations. Take turns asking your group the questions below. Answer with a conditional statement.

Student A: What would you do if you won the lottery?
Student B: If I won the lottery, I'd buy a house.
Student C: If I won the lottery, I'd travel around the world.

What would you do if . . .

1. you had a million dollars?
2. you lived in a mansion?
3. you had your own airplane?
4. you were the boss of a huge company?
5. you owned an island in the Pacific?
6. (your own idea)?

I. **VISUALIZE** Write three statements about what *you* would do if you won the lottery.

1. _____

2. _____

3. _____

GOAL ■ Interpret credit card and loan information

A. Do you have a credit card? What kind of card is it? What is the interest rate? What do you use it for? Discuss these questions with your group.

B. Read the information below about credit cards.

What do I need to know before applying for a credit card?

What is a credit card and how is it different from a debit card? A credit card is a flexible way of borrowing money to make a purchase and paying back the money later. A debit card is a way of taking money directly from your bank account.

Annual fee: Many issuers charge an *annual* fee for using their card—typically between $15 and $50. If you do not plan to pay your bill within a month or two from the date you make a purchase, you should probably look for a card with no annual fee.

Annual percentage rate (APR): APR can be either "fixed" or "variable." Fixed-rate APRs are usually a little higher, but you know exactly how much you will be charged each month.

Introductory rate: Some credit cards offer a low *introductory rate* that switches to a higher rate later. Make sure that you know how long the introductory rate is applicable and what APR the card will carry after the introductory period. Be aware that the introductory rate for some cards will be terminated if you are late with a payment.

Grace period: The *grace period* is the time between the day you make a purchase and the day when interest begins to be charged. For most cards, it is 25 days from the billing date. Many cards have no grace period and you will pay interest from the date you make a purchase.

Other fees: How much is the penalty for being late? How much do you pay if you go over the *credit limit*? How much does your bank charge you for an ATM withdrawal (cash advance fee)? Is the interest rate for cash advances the same or is it higher than the card's "regular" APR? What is your cash advance limit? Answers to all these questions may influence your choice of credit card.

Benefits: A number of issuers offer additional benefits to card members. Rebate cards allow you to earn cash back and discounts on goods and services based on card usage. Frequent flyer cards allow you to earn miles for each dollar charged.

How do issuers evaluate if I am creditworthy?
Issuers determine *creditworthiness* by what are called the three Cs of credit (capacity, collateral, and character). **Capacity** refers to your ability to pay based on your income and existing debt. **Collateral** refers to any assets you have that can secure payment (e.g., your savings or home ownership). **Character** refers to factors such as your payment history and length of employment. The criteria for accepting applicants vary between issuers and credit card products.

C. INFER What do you think these words mean? Use context clues from the reading in Exercise B to figure out their meanings. Discuss the words with a partner.

annual fee	annual percentage rate (APR)	introductory rate
grace period	late fee credit limit	creditworthiness

D. Read the chart and decide which credit card is the best deal for you.

	Verso	Maincard	Explore card (must pay in full each month)	iCard
Annual Fee	$20	$15	$55	$0
APR	15%	14.9%	NA	21%
Introductory Rate (6 months)	2.9%	0%	3.8%	9.9%
Late Fee	$20	$10	$50	$25
Benefits	none	airline miles (one mile for each dollar you spend)	none	cash back (1% of purchases)

E. Which card did you choose? Why?

_____

_____

F. COMPARE What are the advantages and disadvantages of having a credit card? Work in a group to list them.

Advantages	Disadvantages
_____	_____
_____	_____
_____	_____

G. Read the information about loans.

When you decide to purchase something that costs more than you can pay right now, you can put it on your credit card or you can get a loan. A loan from a bank or lending institution is something you have to apply for. You usually have to specify the amount you want to borrow and what kind of purchase you want to make. For large purchases, you usually need collateral, such as your house, your business, or a down payment. The interest rate will vary according to the amount you borrow, where you borrow the money from, and your creditworthiness.

H. **DIFFERENTIATE** With a partner, discuss the differences between these purchasing options. Make notes in the chart.

Loan	Credit card

I. Look at the list of items. For each item, decide if you should get a loan or put it on a credit card. Discuss your answers with a group.

	Car	College course	TV	Computer	Airline ticket	Small business
loan						
credit card						

LESSON 4 How they pull you in

GOAL ■ Analyze advertising techniques

A. Look at the ads for tablets.

BRAND NEW!

ZONE 2000

7" TOUCH SCREEN
WITH 1280 X 800 RESOLUTION
8GB STORAGE CAPACITY
FRONT AND REAR CAMERAS
FAMILY LIBRARY SHARING

$149.99
INCLUDES FREE COVER

BEST DEAL!
$199.99

NIKEN RS7

8.4" TOUCH SCREEN
WITH 2560 X 1600 RESOLUTION

16GB STORAGE CAPACITY

WI-FI

BLUETOOTH

GREAT FOR YOUR TEENAGER!

ONLY
$49.99

DIGIBOOK 4500

• 7" TOUCH SCREEN
  WITH 1024 X 600 RESOLUTION

• 4GB STORAGE CAPACITY

• WI-FI

• BLUETOOTH

COMES WITH EXTRA CHARGER

GREAT FOR LISTENING TO MUSIC AND WATCHING MOVIES!

TAB X5

•10.1" LED-BACKLIT DISPLAY
 WITH 1920 X 1200 RESOLUTION

•32GB STORAGE CAPACITY

•WI-FI

•DIGITAL SOUND

$199.99

B. ANALYZE Answer the questions. Then, discuss these questions with a group and compare answers.

1. Which ad is the most attractive to you? Why?

_____

2. What kind of information do the ads give?

_____

3. What information is not included?

_____

4. How do the ads try to persuade you to buy the products?

_____

C. IDENTIFY Complete the chart with information from the ads on page 47. If the information is missing from the ad, write *doesn't say*.

	Zone	Niken	Digibook	Tab
Price	149.99	$199.99	49.99	199.99
Screen size	7"	8.4"	7"	10.1"
Resolution	1280 × 800	2500 × 1600	1024 × 600	1920 × 1200
Bluetooth	doesn't say	✓	✓	doesn't say
Storage capacity	8	16	4	32GB
Extras	Camara, Cover	Wifi	extra charger	Digital Sound

D. Is there anything else that you would like to know about the tablets? Write three questions that you might ask a salesperson.

1. _____

2. _____

3. _____

E. DECIDE Based on the advertisements, which tablet would you buy?

F. Discuss these questions with a group.

1. What do advertisers do to get you interested in their products?

2. Can you always trust advertisements?

3. What's the best way to find out the truth about a product?

G. Study the chart with your classmates and teacher.

Passive Voice: Present Tense				
Subject	***Be***	**Past participle**		**Explanation**
Ads	are	written	to sell products.	Since we know that ads are written by advertisers, the information "by advertisers" is not important.
The tablet	is	advertised	on television.	Since we know that the store is advertising the tablet, the information "by the store" is not important.

We use the passive voice to emphasize the object of the action or when the doer is not important.

H. Complete each sentence with the passive voice form of the verbs in parentheses. Make sure you use the correct form of the verb *Be*.

1. Special offers _____ (make) to consumers.

2. Some advertising techniques _____ (use) in order to confuse the buyer.

3. Many products _____ (sell) because of ads.

4. The truth about a product _____ (discover) by doing research and talking to other people who have bought the same product.

5. Often, consumers _____ (trick) into buying a product that they don't really need.

I. With a small group, discuss the statements above.

J. DESIGN Imagine that you and a group of students are part of an advertising firm. Choose a product to write an ad for. Try to persuade people to buy your product. Use some passive voice sentences in your ad! Share your ad with the class.

LESSON ⑤ Express yourself!

GOAL ■ Write a business letter

A. RECALL Tell your classmates about a time when you complained about a product or service.

B. VISUALIZE Read each situation below. Answer the questions with a partner.

1. You got home from the grocery store and realized the milk is sour. Who would you talk to?

   the grocery store manager

   What would you say? *I just got home and realized this milk is sour.*

   What would you like to see happen? *I would like a new carton of milk.*

2. You took a suit to the dry cleaners and it came back with a stain on it. Who would you talk to?

   _____

   What would you say? _____

   What would you like to see happen? _____

3. You paid cash for your meal in a restaurant, but the server did not bring back your change.

   Who would you talk to? _____

   _____

   What would you say? _____

   What would you like to see happen? _____

4. There is a charge on your credit card bill for something that you didn't buy. Who would you talk to?

   _____

   What would you say? _____

   What would you like to see happen? _____

   _____

C. With a partner, choose a situation in Exercise B. Write a conversation between the customer and the representative of the business. Practice your conversation and present it to the class.

D. One of the most effective ways to complain about a product or service is to write a business letter. Read the letter below.

4925 Back Bay Road
Costa Mesa, CA 92627
November 3, 2015

ATTN: Restaurant Manager
Little Italy
58946 Jamboree Road
Irvine, CA 92714

To Whom It May Concern:

    I have been a customer at your restaurant many times and usually the food and service are wonderful. However, last night I was there having dinner with my husband and we had a terrible experience. First of all, our server, Kimberly, greeted us, took our order, and then never returned. When we finally tracked her down, forty minutes later, she was bringing our food, which was cold because it had been sitting in the kitchen too long. We never did get our drinks. When we were finished, we had to find another food server to get our check. We spent two hours at your restaurant and had bad service and a bad meal.

    We have really enjoyed eating at your restaurant in the past so I hope you will take this letter seriously and do more training with your staff.

Sincerely,

Sara Lindgren

Sara Lindgren

E. Answer the questions about the letter.

1. Who is Sara complaining to? _____

2. What is she complaining about? _____

3. What do you think will happen? _____

F. Use these words to label the parts of the business letter on page 51.

- return address
- date
- address
- greeting/salutation

- body
- closing
- typed/printed name
- signature

G. A business letter should contain certain information. Look at Sara's letter again. Did she mention all of these pieces of information in her letter? Highlight the parts of the letter that provide the information.

- who she is
- why she is writing
- an explanation of the problem or situation
- a satisfactory resolution

H. COMPOSE Choose one of these situations and write a business letter to make a complaint. Don't forget to format the letter correctly and include all of the necessary information.

Company	Reason for letter
1. Lane's Accessories 8695 Tiguk Ave. Sioux Falls, SD 57104	The purse you bought is falling apart after one month.
2. Media Vision 4679 Lolly Lane Long Beach, CA 90745	You were charged for two months of cable instead of one.
3. Riverview Bank 47986 Washington Ave. Grand Rapids, MI 49503	There is a charge on your credit card statement that doesn't belong to you.
4. Produce World 875 7th Ave. New York, NY 10011	You were treated poorly by an employee.
5. (your own idea)	(your own idea)

▶ # Compare before you decide

Before You Watch

A. **Look at the picture. Complete each sentence.**

1. Mrs. Smith is teaching a class

   about _____.

2. She is holding a _____.

3. Credit cards have different

   _____.

While You Watch

B. ▶ **Watch the video. Complete the chart.**

	Card A	Card B	Card C
Annual percentage rate	20%		
Annual fee			
Late fee			

Check Your Understanding

C. **Complete the dialog.**

Mateo: Oh … I see. But the one on the left has no annual fee. But the (1) ___APR___ is 20%.

Mrs. Smith: And 20% is fairly high. *If* you had a balance of $100 dollars, you would have to pay

$20 dollars in (2) _____ over the course of a year. Now, what about the one in the middle, Hector?

Hector: That's the best one.

Mrs. Smith: Why is (3) _____?

Hector: Well, the APR is 14%. That doesn't sound too bad. There's a low rate for

(4) _____ and there isn't any annual fee.

Mrs. Smith: If you got this card, you would pay the lowest overall (5) _____.

Review

A. Imagine that your family of four has $3,000 to live on per month. Realistically, how would you budget your money? Fill in the chart.

Monthly expense	Budgeted amount
Rent / Mortgage Payment	
Utilities	
Auto: Car Payment / Gas / Insurance	
Food	
Medical	
Clothing	
Entertainment	
TOTAL	$3,000

B. Look at the budget below. Calculate the differences and totals.

Monthly Expense		Budgeted Amount	Actual Amount Spent	Difference
Auto	Car Payment	$404.00	$404.00	
	Insurance	$72.39	$72.39	
	Gas	$180.00	$179.90	
	Maintenance	$100.00	$29.99	
Housing	House Payment	$1,490.00	$1,490.00	
	Utilities	$122.00	$110.75	
	Phone (home, cell)	$150.00	$230.00	
Food	Groceries	$350.00	$345.00	
	Eating Out	$200.00	$215.00	
Other	Clothing	$350.00	$224.59	
	Entertainment	$300.00	$315.03	
	Medical	$100.00	$40.00	
	TOTAL			

C. What are three things you can do to be a smart consumer?

1. _____

2. _____

3. _____

D. Imagine that you have just inherited $100,000 from a relative. What would you do with it? Write three conditional statements about the possibilities. Then, share your answers with the class.

1. If I inherited $100,000, I would _____

2. _____

3. _____

E. Write *credit card*, *loan*, or *both* for each statement.

1. You need to apply for this.   _____

2. This can be used to buy an expensive item.   _____

3. You need collateral for this.   _____

4. This often has an annual fee.   _____

5. Sometimes this has an introductory offer.   _____

6. You will pay a penalty if your payment is late. _____

7. This has an interest rate that affects your payments. _____

8. You can get this from the bank.   _____

F. List three advertising techniques that are used to get you to buy a product.

1. _____

2. _____

3. _____

G. Imagine that you are writing an advertisement for a product. What information should be included in your ad? Make a list and share it with the class.

_____

_____

_____

_____

_____

_____

H. Complete each sentence with the passive form of the verb in parentheses.

1. Tablets _____ (sell) at electronics stores.

2. Advertisements _____ (create) to sell products.

3. Advertisers _____ (pay) to convince you to buy certain products.

4. Sometimes an ad _____ (write) to confuse you.

I. What four things should be included in a business letter that expresses a complaint?

1. _____   2. _____

3. _____   4. _____

J. Decide if each statement is True or False based on what you learned in this unit. If the statement is False, rewrite it to make it True.

_____ 1. A smart consumer asks a lot of questions about a product before buying it.

_____

_____ 2. Advertisements always tell you everything about the product.

_____

_____ 3. Budgets are only for people with a lot of money.

_____

_____ 4. It is better to pay cash for something if you can.

_____

_____ 5. Sometimes credit cards carry high interest rates.

_____

K. Make your own dictionary of the new words that you are learning in this class. Make a list of 12 words that were new to you. Put them in alphabetical order in your notebook.

1. Buy a ruled notebook.

2. Divide the notebook into 26 sections—one for each letter of the alphabet.

3. As you learn new words, write them in your dictionary in the correct section.

4. After each word, write the page number where the word appears in your book, the definition, and an example sentence.

TEAM PROJECT ✓ **Create a purchase plan**

With a team, create a purchase plan for a large item. Think of the steps you should follow and how to implement these.

1. **COLLABORATE** Form a team with four or five students. Choose positions for each member of your team:

Position	Job description	Student name
Student 1: **Team Leader**	Check that everyone speaks English and participates.	
Student 2: **Secretary**	Take notes. Write down purchase plan.	
Student 3: **Designer**	Design ad for product and purchase plan layout.	
Students 4: **Spokesperson**	Report information to the class. Prepare team for the presentation.	
Students 5: **Assistant**	Help the secretary and designer with their work.	

2. Decide on a large item that your team would like to purchase.

3. Create an advertisement for this product.

4. Write down all the steps you will need to take to purchase this item. (*Hint:* Think about a budget, comparison shopping, ads, and loan information.)

5. Write a brief description of how you will complete each step.

6. Design a purchase plan poster that has a space for the ad, each step in your purchase plan, and artwork.

7. Present your purchase plan to the class.

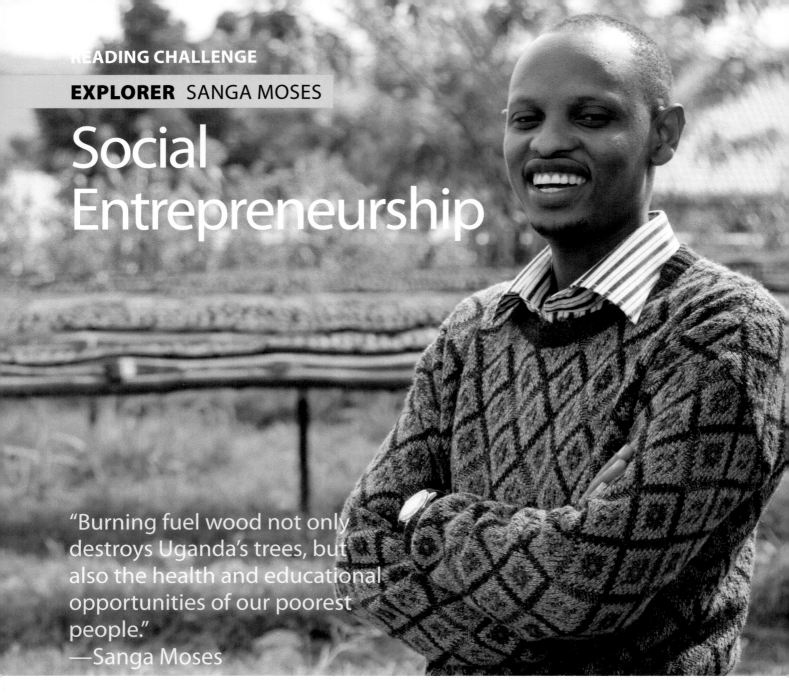

EXPLORER SANGA MOSES

Social Entrepreneurship

"Burning fuel wood not only destroys Uganda's trees, but also the health and educational opportunities of our poorest people."
—Sanga Moses

A. Discuss the vocabulary below. Then, match each word to its definition.

1. kiln
2. briquette
3. food waste
4. fuel
5. air pollution
6. respiratory disease
7. clean burning

a. burns without contamination
b. stove
c. illness in the lungs
d. air that is contaminated
e. things that get thrown away
f. form of fuel used for burning
g. a substance that when burned produces heat

B. Read about Sanga Moses.

Sanga Moses had a dream: He wanted to give clean, cheap, cooking energy to all Africans. He also wanted to reduce air pollution and decrease the likelihood of respiratory disease. So, he quit his job in Uganda and started working with engineering students. They designed kilns and briquetting machines that could turn food waste into fuel. Today, over 115,000 Ugandans use this clean-burning fuel every day. Not only did he create a way to help the environment, but he found a way to put money in the pockets of his fellow countrymen. Read what Sanga did, in his own words.

How did you get started in your field of work?

In 2009, I traveled from Kampala to go and visit my mother in my village. While walking home, I saw my 12-year-old sister carrying a heavy bundle of firewood on her head. She told me that she had missed school because she had to gather firewood. She also said she was tired of missing school to gather wood and started to cry. This upset me because I wanted my sister to stay in school. So, I decided to quit my job and focus on finding a solution to the problem—overdependence on fuelwood in sub-Saharan Africa. That way girls like my sister could stay in school. Everyone thought I was crazy!

What has been your most rewarding or memorable experience in your field?

The progress we have achieved so far has been very rewarding. Today, there are 2,500 farmers who use our kilns. These farmers also make extra income—up to $30 a month each. We have created a network of 460 women retailers who sell our clean cooking fuel. Each of these retailers earns up to $150 a month in extra income, and over 19,167 households, or about 115,000 people, now use our clean cooking fuel on a daily basis. The progress we have made so far has been very rewarding.

C. Answer the following questions based on the reading.

1. How much extra money can a farmer make by using a kiln? _____

2. How many women retailers are selling this fuel? _____

3. Why is this cooking fuel so important? _____

_____

D. VISUALIZE Imagine you are a farmer using a kiln or a retailer selling cooking fuel. Write a business e-mail to Sanga Moses, thanking him for what he has done. Don't forget the parts of a business e-mail.

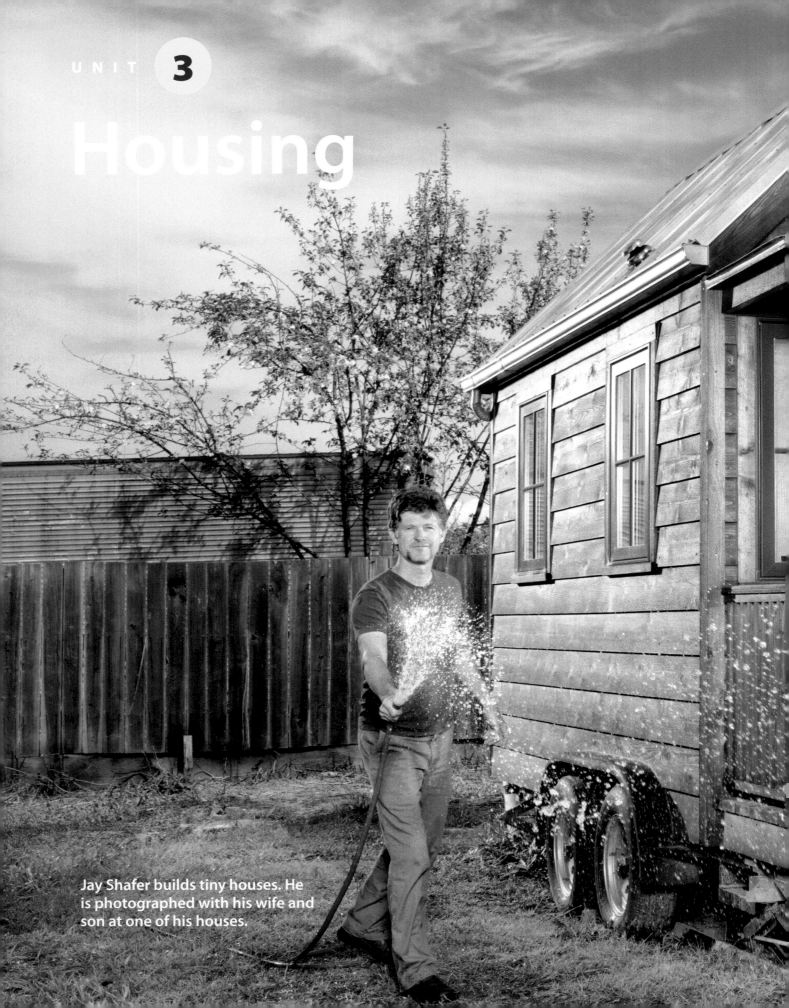

UNIT **3**

Housing

Jay Shafer builds tiny houses. He is photographed with his wife and son at one of his houses.

UNIT OUTCOMES

- ☐ Interpret housing advertisements
- ☐ Compare types of housing
- ☐ Identify housing preferences
- ☐ Identify the steps to buying a home
- ☐ Interpret mortgage information

Look at the photo and answer the questions.

1. What is happening in the picture?
2. What is special about the type of housing?
3. What do you need to buy a house like this?

GOAL ■ Interpret housing advertisements

A. IDENTIFY **Read the advertisements of homes for sale. Write the type of home above the correct description.**

| Suburban Dream | Country Cottage | Downtown Condominium |

HOMES FOR SALE

Cozy two-bedroom, two-bath, single-family home. Located in a secluded neighborhood, far from city life.

You won't believe this price for a house in this area. Working fireplace. Big yard. Excellent seasonal views. Must sell. Come see and make an offer now!

$240,000

Single-family, 4-bedroom, 3-bath, 2,500 sq. ft. home with an added family room. Needs some loving care.

Location is great!

Near jobs, bus, and schools. You must see this home and area. Amenities: pool, fireplace, central a/c, built-in master suite, and big yard!

Let's negotiate!

Asking price $325,000

This 1,000- square-foot condo is owned by the original owner and you'd think it was brand-new! Located in the heart of Los Angeles near all the nightlife you could imagine. Seller just added new carpet, new paint, new faucets and sinks, and beautiful ceramic tile flooring. Two master suites, indoor laundry room, detached two-car garage, and large patio area. This condo will not last long on the market, so hurry!

$300,000

B. DEFINE Real estate agents write advertisements to get you excited about a property. What do you think the following phrases from the ads could mean? Write your own definitions.

asking price	Negociete
brand-new	New house
cozy	Confortable
master suite	Hotel ?
near nightlife	Downg town
needs loving care	Remodelecion
seasonal views	Good view
secluded	Alone

C. INFER The words in the box describe the process of buying a home. Find each word in the ads on page 62 and work out the meaning by using the context. Discuss the meanings with a partner.

offer	market	negotiate	amenities

D. Look back at the ads on page 62 and complete the chart.

	Type of Property	Size	Asking Price	Number of Bedrooms	Number of Bathrooms	Location	Amenities
Country Cottage	Single-family home	?	240K	2	2	Secluded neighborhood	big yard, fireplace, view
Suburban Dream	single-family home	2.500 sq. Ft	325K	4	3	great locacion	Pool, fireplace, big Yard
Downtown Condominium		1,000 sq. ft.	300K	2	2	L.A. Angeles	2 Car garage, laundry Patio area

E. Listen to the advertisements of homes for sale and fill in the information you hear.

CD 1
TR 9

Prince's Palace
Price: _____
Size: _____
Neighborhood:
_____
Amenities: _____
_____

Fixer-Upper
Price: _____
Size: _____
Neighborhood:
_____
Amenities: _____
_____

City High-Rise
Price: _____
Size: _____
Neighborhood:
_____
Amenities: _____
_____

Rural Residence
Price: _____
Size: _____
Neighborhood:
_____
Amenities: _____
_____

F. **COMPOSE** Use the vocabulary you have learned in this lesson to write an advertisement for the place where you live now. Draw or paste in a picture.

LESSON 2 Bigger? Better?

GOAL ▪ Compare types of housing

🎧 **A.** **Listen to Joey and Courtney discuss two properties that Courtney looked at. As you
CD 1
TR 10** **listen, take notes about the advantages and disadvantages of each place.**

House	Advantages	Disadvantages
	closer to job	
Condominium		

B. **COMPARE** **With a partner, compare the house and the condominium.**

    Student A: What's an advantage of living in the house?
    Student B: The house is larger than the condo.

C. **JUSTIFY** **Which one would you rather live in? Why? Explain your reasons to a partner.**

D. **Complete the lists with a partner.**

Adjective	Comparative	Superlative
beautiful	more beautiful	the most beautiful
noisy	noisier	the noisiest
safe	Safier	The safiers
comfortable	more Comfortable	The most Confortable
far	farth /further	the furthers
friendly	Friendlyer	The friendlyers
cheap	Cheaper	The Cheaperst
big	Bigger	The Biggerst

*Note: Some two-syllable adjectives have two forms; for example, *quieter* or *more quiet*.

E. **INFER** What are the rules? Write the adjective(s) from Exercise D that corresponds to each rule.

1. Add **-er** or **-est** to one-syllable adjectives.
   _____cheap_____

2. Use **more** or **the most** before two-syllable adjectives.
   _____

3. Add **-r** or **-st** to one-syllable adjectives that end in **e**.
   _____

4. Change **y** to **i** and add **-er** or **-est**.
   _____

5. Some adjectives have irregular forms.
   _____

6. Double the final consonant of adjectives ending in the pattern of consonant-vowel-consonant and add **-er** or **-est**.
   _____

F. **COMPARE** Describe the place you live in now and compare your house to a friend's or family member's house. Use the adjectives from Exercise D.

I live in a two bedroom apartment. My cousin lives in a three bedroom house. His house is bigger than mine.

G. Listen to Sara and Courtney talk about homes that Sara has looked at recently.

CD 1
TR 11

Courtney:	Have you looked at any new houses this week?
Sara:	Yes, I looked at three places the other day. Look at this brochure!
Courtney:	The *Country Cottage,* the *Suburban Dream,* and the *Downtown Condominium.* I like the sound of the *Country Cottage* best. It sounds more comfortable than the others.
Sara:	Yeah, and it's the closest to where we live now.
Courtney:	Oh, really? Which place is the safest?
Sara:	Actually, I think the *Suburban Dream* is the safest.
Courtney:	Which one has the biggest floor plan?
Sara:	The *Suburban Dream*. It would be ideal for our family.
Courtney:	Is it the most expensive?
Sara:	Why, of course! I have expensive taste.

H. **What questions does Courtney ask? How does Sara answer her? Practice the conversation with a partner.**

I. **Study the charts with your teacher.**

Questions Using Comparative and Superlative Adjectives				
Question word	**Subject**	**Verb**	**Adjective or noun**	**Rule**
Which	one place house	is	bigger? closer to work? the safest?	Use *be* when following the verb with an adjective.
		has	more rooms? the biggest floor plan?	Use *have* before a noun.

Long and Short Answers			
Question	**Short answer**	**Long answer**	**Rules**
Which one is bigger, the condominium or the house?	The condominium.	The condominium is bigger. The condominium is bigger *than* the house.	• When talking about two things and mentioning both of them, use *than*.
Which place has more rooms?	The house.	The house has more rooms. The house has more rooms *than* the condominium.	• When talking about two things, but only mentioning one of them, do not use *than*.

J. **Write four comparative questions about the homes Joey and Courtney talked about in Exercise A.**

1. _Which place is closer to Courtney's job?_____
2. _____
3. _____
4. _____
5. _____

K. **With a partner, practice asking and answering the questions you wrote in Exercise J.**

L. **COMPARE** **Write sentences on a piece of paper comparing a place you used to live in to the place you live in now.**

My old house had more bedrooms than the house I live in now.

LESSON ③ Housing preferences

GOAL ■ Identify housing preferences

🎧 **A.** **Think about these questions as you listen to the story about the Bwarie family.**

CD 1
TR 12

1. Why is the Bwarie family looking for a new home?

2. What are they looking for in a new home?

The Bwarie family has outgrown their apartment. They have three children and a baby on the way, and they are now renting a two-bedroom house. They've been putting away money every month from their paychecks, and they finally have enough money for a down payment on a house. Every Sunday, the whole family piles into the car and goes to look at properties for sale. So far, they have been doing this on their own, but now it's time to find a realtor.

However, before they meet with a realtor, they need to decide exactly what they want. Courtney and Joey Bwarie have thought long and hard about what they want to purchase. First of all, they want a house in a safe neighborhood that is within walking distance to the school that their children attend. Second of all, they want four bedrooms, one for Courtney and Joey, one for the two boys, and another for their daughter and the baby girl who will be born next month. The fourth room will be used as an office for Courtney, who works out of the home. As far as bathrooms, four would be ideal, but they could survive with three if they had to. Some other things they would like are a big backyard for the children to play in and an attached two-car garage. Other amenities, such as air-conditioning or a pool, are not important to them.

Now, they know what they are looking for in a new home. That was the easy part. Finding the home . . . that's a different story!

B. **INFER** **Read the story again. Work out the meanings of these words and expressions by using the context.**

down payment	on the way	outgrown
pile into	putting away	realtor
within walking distance	works out of the home	ideal
survive	thought long and hard	

C. **APPLY** **Go over the meanings of the words and expressions with your teacher. Then, choose three of the words or expressions and use them in sentences.**

D. SPECIFY What are the Bwaries looking for in a home? Complete the checklist with as much information as you can based on the story in Exercise A.

Housing Preferences Checklist				
Features	Yes	No	Features	Preference
air-conditioning	☐	☐	type of property	
backyard	☐	☐	number of bathrooms	
balcony	☐	☐	number of bedrooms	
garage	☐	☐	location	
heating	☐	☐	price range	
pool	☐	☐	down payment (percentage)	

E. What information on the checklist did the Bwaries not talk about? What do you think their preferences might be regarding these items?

F. When asking someone about their preferences, you can use *yes/no* questions. Study the chart below.

Yes/No Questions and Answers		
Do you want	air-conditioning? a backyard?	Yes, I do. No, I don't.
Do they need	a balcony? a garage?	Yes, they do. No, they don't.
Does the house have	heating? a pool?	Yes, it does. No, it doesn't.

G. Practice asking and answering *yes/no* questions with a partner. Use the information in Exercise D.

Student A: Do they want air-conditioning?
Student B: No, they don't.

> **YES/NO QUESTIONS**
>
> *Rising Intonation*
>
> Do you want a yard?
>
> Do you want five bedrooms?
>
> Does the house have a pool?
>
> Does it have a balcony?

H. Information questions start with *who, what, where, when, why,* or *how*. Study the chart.

Information Questions			
Information	**Example Questions**		
type of property	What type	of property	do you want? is it?
number of bathrooms number of bedrooms	How many	bedrooms bathrooms	do you want? does it have?
location	Where		is it?
price range	What		is your price range?
down payment (percentage)	How much		can you put down?

I. Practice asking and answering information questions with a partner. Use the information from the chart in Exercise D.

Student A: What type of property do they want?
Student B: They want a house.

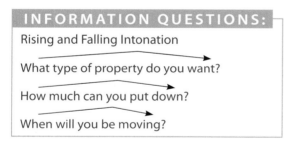

INFORMATION QUESTIONS:

Rising and Falling Intonation

What type of property do you want?

How much can you put down?

When will you be moving?

J. DETERMINE and COMPARE   What would *you* like in a new home? Look at the checklist in Exercise D and make your own list of housing preferences. You might want to add some extra things that are not on the list. Compare your list with a partner.

LESSON 4 Step-by-step

GOAL   Identify the steps to buying a home

A.   What are some ways to find a house? With a group, list your ideas.

B.   Read the letter that Joey wrote to Paradise Realty.

15236 Dahlia Avenue
Costa Mesa, CA 92627
February 13, 2016

Paradise Realty
9875 Timber Lane
Costa Mesa, CA 92627

Dear Paradise Realty:

My family has decided to purchase a new home, and we would appreciate any information you can send us about homes for sale.

We are looking for a four-bedroom home. We would like to live in a safe neighborhood, close to our children's school. We would prefer a home with a big enclosed yard that our children can play in. We might want to build a pool in the future, but right now it is not a priority. Other amenities, such as air-conditioning, central heating, and closet space would be nice, but they are not essential.

Our price range is between $300,000 and $350,000, and we are prepared to put down 10%. Please contact me at the address above or you may call me or my wife, Courtney, at (949) 555-2408. Thank you for your time.

Sincerely,

Joseph Bwarie

Joseph Bwarie

C. PUT IN ORDER Read the steps for buying a home and number them in the correct order.

_____ Apply for a loan.

_____ Choose a home you'd like to buy.

_____ Decide how much money you can spend.

_____ Decide what you are looking for.

_____ Have the home inspected.

_____ Make an offer on the home.

_____ Move in.

_____ Negotiate until both parties come to an agreement.

_____ Start looking for homes in a neighborhood you'd like to live in.

D. Now, read the article about home buying and check your answers.

BUYING A HOME

Home buyers can spend up to three months, and possibly more, looking for and purchasing a home. Their search begins by looking at housing ads, driving through neighborhoods they are interested in, and walking through open houses. Many first-time buyers will meet with a real estate agent to get help finding and buying a home.

Home buyers should know how much they can afford before they start looking for a home. It isn't worth your time to look for a new home if you can't really afford to buy one. So, it's a good idea to look at your financial situation first. You might be surprised how much money you can borrow, especially if the interest rates are good. Also, if you have some money for a down payment, your monthly payments may be lower than you think.

You should never make an offer on a home without looking at other houses in the same neighborhood. Just as you would comparison shop for a car or computer, you should do a cost comparison on different homes for sale. You can do this by asking about the recent sales of similar properties, which any real estate agent can tell you. Also, if you can find something out about the seller and his or her motivation for selling, it will put you in a better position to negotiate. For instance, maybe the seller needs to sell quickly and would accept a low offer.

Once you have found the property that you want and can afford, you are ready to make an offer. A low-ball offer is an offer that is much lower than the asking price. Unless the house is really overpriced or the seller needs to sell it quickly, he or she will probably not accept a low-ball offer. Once you make an offer that is reasonable to the seller, he or she will either accept it or make a counteroffer. If he or she makes a counteroffer, the negotiating process has begun. You may have to go back three or four times before an agreement is reached.

Being a good negotiator can be tricky. Take your time when making your decision. This is a very important decision and you don't want to be rushed. Sometimes you can negotiate for repairs to be done to the home before you move in, or you can ask the seller to pay for some of your closing costs. As soon as a written offer is made and accepted by both parties, the document becomes a legally binding contract.

One of the first things you do after the contract is agreed upon is to get a home inspection. You need to hire a paid professional inspector to inspect the home, searching for defects or other problems. The inspector usually represents the buyer and is paid for by the buyer. The contract that you sign with the seller protects you as a buyer by allowing you to cancel closing on the deal if an inspector finds problems with the property that the seller is unwilling to have fixed or give the buyer credit for.

Once the contract has been signed, the lender (usually a bank) starts processing the loan. Once all the inspections are done and any repairs are completed, the final papers for the transfer of the title are prepared. Finally, the closing takes place on the date agreed upon in the offer. On that date, the title comes to you and you can begin enjoying your new home!

E. **INFER** Find these words in the article and match them with the correct meaning.

_____ 1. afford   a. a legal document

_____ 2. contract   b. amount of money that buyer is willing to pay for a house

_____ 3. cost comparison   c. looking at different prices of homes

_____ 4. negotiate   d. person or company that loans money

_____ 5. lender   e. the desire to do something

_____ 6. motivation   f. when all papers are signed and titles are transferred

_____ 7. offer   g. to have enough money to purchase something

_____ 8. closing   h. discuss until you reach an agreement

F. With a partner, discuss the benefits and the drawbacks of owning your own home.

G. **SUMMARIZE** Write a paragraph summarizing the process of buying a home.

_____

_____

_____

_____

_____

GOAL ▪ Interpret mortgage information

A. Todd and Sara Mason are thinking of buying a house. Todd is worried about money, so he made an appointment with a financial planner to talk about a mortgage. Discuss the questions below with a partner.

1. What is a financial planner?

2. What do you think the financial planner will tell Todd about getting a mortgage? Make a list with a partner.

1.
2.
3.
4.
5.
6.
7.

B. Listen to Todd talk to the financial planner. What does the financial planner say? Is anything he says on the list you made?

CD 1
TR 13

C. DEFINE Do you know what these words and expressions mean? Discuss them with your classmates and teacher.

mortgage	financial commitment	afford
get approved for a loan	price range	credit check
down payment	deposit	purchase price

🎧 **D.** Listen to the first part of the conversation again. What are the three questions Todd
CD 1
TR 14
must ask himself? Write them below.

1. _____

2. _____

3. _____

🎧 **E.** Listen to what the financial planner says and write the next four steps Todd must
CD 1
TR 15
take below.

1. _____

2. _____

3. _____

4. _____

🎧 **F.** Todd will need to give the financial planner six things. Do you remember what they
CD 1
TR 16
are? Write them below. If you can't remember, listen again.

1. _____

2. _____

3. _____

4. _____

5. _____

6. _____

G. Imagine that you are trying to get a mortgage and you have to gather all of the
items listed in Exercise F. Put a checkmark (✓) next to each one that you have at
home right now.

H. Now that Todd knows how to get a mortgage, he needs to learn about the different types of mortgages. Read about each type below.

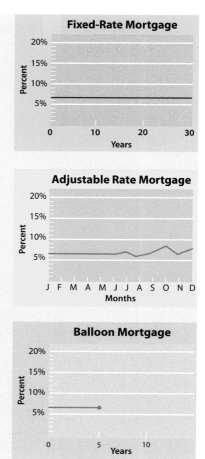

Fixed-Rate Mortgages

A fixed-rate mortgage has a fixed interest rate for the life of the loan, which could be 10, 20, or 30 years. You will make the same payment every month for the life of the loan and, at the end of the term, your loan will be paid off. The advantage of this type of loan is the interest rate never changes and the monthly payment is always the same.

Adjustable Rate Mortgages

An adjustable rate mortgage (ARM) begins like a fixed-rate mortgage with a fixed interest rate and a constant monthly payment, but this mortgage will adjust after a certain amount of time, anywhere from six months to five years. At this point, the interest rate and your monthly payment will change based on the market at the time. Furthermore, every month the rate and payment could change based on how the market changes.

Balloon Mortgages

A balloon mortgage has a fixed interest rate and a fixed monthly payment, but after a certain amount of time, for example five years, the entire balance of the loan is due. This is a short-term loan, usually for people who can't qualify for a fixed-rate mortgage or an ARM.

I. **CLASSIFY** Using the information from Exercise H, put a checkmark (✓) in the correct column(s).

	Fixed-Rate	ARM	Balloon
1. The monthly payment is always the same.			
2. The interest rate changes after a certain period of time.			
3. The interest rate is fixed.			
4. The monthly payment will change based on the market.			
5. This type of loan is short-term.			

J. **SUPPOSE** If you were going to buy a house, which type of loan would you get? Why? Write a short paragraph about your preference.

LIFESKILLS 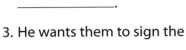 We are going to be roommates

Before You Watch

A. Look at the picture. Complete each sentence.

1. Naomi, Hector, and Mateo are moving into their new _____.

2. Mr. Thomas is their new

   _____.

3. He wants them to sign the

   _____.

While You Watch

B. ▶ **Watch the video. Complete the chart.**

Length of lease	12 months
Rent	
Deposit (before the administrative fee)	
Administrative Fee	
Cleaning Deposit	
Total Deposit	

Check Your Understanding

C. Put the words in order to make well-formed questions.

1. much / the / is / rent / how

   _____

2. deposit / is / much / how / the

   _____

3. long / how / lease / the / is

   _____

4. fees / any / other / there / are

   _____

5. copy / of / lease / the / have / can / I / a

   _____

Review

A. Read the housing advertisements and complete the chart below.

1. Always wanted to take a house and make it your own? Settle into this 4-bedroom, 3.5 ba, 2,000-square-foot fixer-upper. $250,000. Located in a busy neighborhood with lots of other families, this place is perfect for a young family.

2. Move out of the slow life and into the fast lane! Check out this beautifully spacious 1,200-square-foot studio apartment at the top of one of the city's newest sky rises. 2 bedrooms, 1 bathroom. The building has 24-hour security. Utility room with washers and dryers is in the basement. The owner wants to lease it for $2,000 a month but will sell it for $700,000. Hurry! This one will go fast!

	Type of Property	Size	Asking Price	Number of Bedrooms	Number of Bathrooms	Location	Amenities
Home #1							
Home #2							

B. Using the ads above, complete the following sentences by circling the correct verb and using comparatives and superlatives.

1. Home #1 (is / has) _____ than Home #2. (space)

2. Home #1 (is / has) _____. (expensive)

3. Home #2 (is / has) _____ than Home #1. (big)

4. Home #2 (is / has) _____. (security)

5. Home #1 (is / has) _____ than Home #2. (spacious)

6. Home #1 (is / has) _____ than Home #2. (small)

Learner Log

I can complete a housing preferences checklist.   I can explain the steps to buying a home.
  ☐ Yes   ☐ Maybe   ☐ No   ☐ Yes   ☐ Maybe   ☐ No

C. Complete the housing preferences checklist based on what you would want in a home.

Housing Preferences Checklist				
Features	**Yes**	**No**	**Features**	**Preference**
air-conditioning	☐	☐	type of property	
backyard	☐	☐	number of bathrooms	
garage	☐	☐	number of bedrooms	
heating	☐	☐	location	
pool	☐	☐	price range	

D. Write three *yes/no* questions you could ask someone about his or her housing preferences.

1. _____

2. _____

3. _____

E. Write three information questions you could ask someone about his or her housing preferences.

1. _____

2. _____

3. _____

F. **Now, ask a partner the questions you wrote in Exercises D and E and complete the checklist below based on his or her answers.**

Housing Preferences Checklist				
Features	Yes	No	Features	Preference
air-conditioning	☐	☐	type of property	
backyard	☐	☐	number of bathrooms	
garage	☐	☐	number of bedrooms	
heating	☐	☐	location	
pool	☐	☐	price range	

G. **Put the steps to buying a home in the correct order (1–10).**

_____ Start looking at ads in the newspaper and looking in neighborhoods you'd like to live in.

_____ Negotiate with the seller until you come to an agreement.

_____ Move in.

_____ Make an offer on a home.

_____ Get the title to the house transferred into your name.

_____ Get a home inspection.

_____ Find the home you want to buy.

_____ Figure out how much money you can spend.

_____ Decide on your housing preferences.

_____ Apply for a loan.

H. **Take turns describing the process of getting a mortgage with a partner.**

I. **It is helpful to create lists of words that are related so you can recall them. In this unit, you learned new words related to buying a home. Complete the lists below with related words from this unit in your notebook.**

Housing ads	Buying a home	Mortgages
cozy	home inspection	fixed-rate

☑ # Create a real estate brochure and decide on a property to buy

With a team, create a purchase plan for a large item. Think of the steps you should follow and how to implement these.

COLLABORATE Form a team with four or five students. Choose roles for each member of your team.

Position	Job description	Student name
Student 1: **Team Leader**	Check that everyone speaks English and participates.	
Student 2: **Writer**	Write advertisements. Write list of preferences and questions.	
Student 3: **Designer**	Design a brochure.	
Students 4/5: **Realtors**	Represent the real estate agency.	

Part 1: With an advertising team, you will create a real estate brochure.

1. Create an imaginary real estate agency. What is the name of your agency?

2. Come up with three houses that your agency is trying to sell. Make a brochure for these properties, including pictures and brief advertisements. Display your brochure in the classroom.

Part 2: As a family, you will choose which properties you are interested in, meet with a realtor, and decide which property to purchase.

1. As a family, decide what your housing preferences are and make a list.

2. From the brochures posted around the room, choose two properties that you are interested in, each one from a different agency.

3. Prepare a list of questions that you'd like to ask about each property.

4. In teams of two or three, set up appointments with the realtor and meet with them about the properties you are interested in purchasing.

5. Report back to your group and make a decision about which property you'd like to make an offer on.

6. Make an offer on the property.

EXPLORER CALEB HARPER

Changing cities

"My passion comes from wanting to combine the things I love in life: technology, architecture, and engineering with my innate desire to grow things."
—Caleb Harper

heliospectra

A. Look at the pictures above. Work with a small group to identify what each picture is.

B. Make a list of what is ABSOLUTELY NECESSARY in each of these spaces.

URBAN FARM	HOUSE	GARDEN
_____	_____	_____
_____	_____	_____
_____	_____	_____

C. **COMPARE** Share your list with another group.

D. You will see the words *urban farm* and *cargotecture* in the reading. What do you think these words mean?

E. Read the article on changing cities.

Changing cities

Cities are becoming more and more crowded, but just because there are more people doesn't mean there is more space for their needs. Food distribution for large cities is complex and costly. Infrastructure is limited and cities are having to be creative. Here are some innovative ways cities are changing their resources.

Go green

Caleb Harper, an urban agriculturalist, has combined his passion for technology, architecture, and engineering with his interest in growing things. Through several initiatives he has explored ways of ensuring that food production is easily available to cities.

Caleb has suggested several solutions for overcoming the food availability problems. Using aeroponic agriculture, a method of irrigation first developed by NASA, and vertical farms with high production, he suggests cities will have food that is fresher, cheaper, and available all year round. People who live in urban areas will be involved in growing their own food and thus ensure constant supplies and cut costs. He says, "Our ability to produce 365 days a year, as opposed to being dependent on a growing season, also gives them [urban farms] a tremendous advantage."

Live differently

In Amsterdam, for example, housing is starting to look a little different. This Dutch city is very crowded and the need for low-income housing has caused people to think outside of the box. Or maybe inside the box is a better way to put it. The growing practice of "cargotecture," using steel shipping containers for architectural purposes, is being implemented here. They've started taking discarded shipping containers and turning them into homes.

Looking forward

By 2030, over 60% of the population will live in cities, cities that are overcrowded and lack affordable housing and easy access to food supply. So compact housing could be a solution to this lack of space. In addition, growing food in cities and making them self-sufficient will address the food needs of large cities. Can you imagine living in a shipping container? Can you imagine growing your own food?

F. IMAGINE Design an urban farm in your group. Where would you plant? What would you plant? Why? Share your ideas with the class.

G. The internationally standardized (ISO) containers are 40 feet long by 8 feet wide by 8.5 feet high (12.2 by 2.4 by 2.6 meters). With a small group, design a building space using a shipping container.

H. On a separate piece of paper, write an opinion paragraph on why you think growing your own food in urban farms or reusing shipping containers is important.

UNIT **4**

Community

Musicians perform on the beach at the 2013 Mermaid Parade at Coney Island, Brooklyn. Coney Island was hard-hit by Superstorm Sandy, but parade organizers were able to raise $100,000 to fund the parade.

UNIT OUTCOMES

☐ Locate community resources

☐ Use the telephone

☐ Give suggestions

☐ Interpret a road map

☐ Identify ways to volunteer in
the community

**Look at the photo and
answer the questions.**

1. What is happening in
the picture?

2. What are the people
celebrating?

3. How is the community
involved?

LESSON (1) Your community

GOAL ■ Locate community resources

A. **Look at the picture. Where is Consuela? What information can she find at the Loronado Welcome Center? Read the conversation and find out what kind of help she needs.**

Consuela:	Hi. We just moved to <u>Loronado</u> and I'm looking for a place to <u>get a job</u>. Can you help me?
Receptionist:	Of course. Why don't you try the <u>Employment Development Department</u>? It's located on <u>Orange Avenue</u>.
Consuela:	Great! Thanks.

B. **With a partner, practice the conversation in Exercise A, but change the <u>underlined</u> information. Use the expressions below and information you know about your community.**

1. take some English classes
2. get a bus schedule
3. use a computer
4. volunteer
5. check out some books
6. get medical help
7. register my little boy for school
8. go swimming
9. look at some art
10. sign up for baseball

C. **ANALYZE** In each question in the box, there are actually two questions. Can you find them? Write them below.

> Do you know if there is a library near here?
> Can you show me where Orange Avenue is?
> Can you tell me when the post office opens?

1. Do you know if there is a library near here?

   1st question: *Do you know?*

   2nd question: *Is there a library near here?*

2. Can you show me where Orange Avenue is?

   1st question: _____

   2nd question: _____

3. Can you tell me when the post office opens?

   1st question: _____

   2nd question: _____

D. Study the chart. When two questions are combined into one, it is called an *embedded question*. One question is embedded in the other.

Embedded Questions		
Introductory question	**Embedded question**	**Rules**
Can you show me	where **Orange Avenue is?**	In an embedded information question, the subject comes before the verb.
Do you know	*if* there is a library near here?	For *yes/no* questions, use *if* before the embedded question.
Can you tell me	when the library opens?	For questions with *do* or *does,* take out *do/does* and use the verb that agrees with the subject.
Why do we use embedded questions? They sound more polite than direct questions.		

Common Expressions Used to Introduce Embedded Questions	
Would you tell me what time the bank closes?	**Will you show me** where the adult school is?
Can you explain where I drop off my books?	**Do you know** if I can buy a computer there?

E.   Change these questions to embedded questions using the expressions from the box.

1. What is the name of the local adult school?

    Do you know what the name of the local adult school is?

2. What is the address of the public pool?

    _____

3. Where is Loronado?

    _____

4. Do you sell running shoes?

    _____

5. What time does the library close?

    _____

6. Is Orange Adult School on this street?

    _____

7. When do classes begin?

    _____

8. Where do you take your cans and papers for recycling?

    _____

9. Is your restaurant open on Sunday evenings?

    _____

F.   FORMULATE On a piece of paper, write five embedded questions that you could ask a school counselor.

EXAMPLE: **Can you explain how to get a high school diploma?**

LESSON ② Can you tell me . . . ?

GOAL ■ Use the telephone

A. What phone number would you call if you wanted information about the following items? Look at the directory below and write the correct number on the line.

1. getting a driver's license   *555-0013*

2. a bus schedule   _____

3. a place to borrow books   _____

4. medical help   _____

5. school registration for your teenage son   _____

6. swim lessons   _____

7. looking at some art   _____

8. a place for your daughter to skate after school   _____

9. contesting your parking ticket   _____

10. activities for your grandparents   _____

Community Resources

Balboa Park Museum
555-2939   71852 Orange Avenue

Bus Transit
555-2678   35984 First Street

Chamber of Commerce
555-4671   72064 Orange Avenue

City Clerk
555-8403   63246 Fifth Street #1

Department of Motor Vehicles
555-0013   54679 Fourth Street

Employment Development Department
555-5334   94678 Orange Avenue

Health Clinic
555-8473   26489 First Street

High School
555-1238   34658 Loro Road

Hospital
555-7623   79346 Orange Avenue

Little League Baseball
555-7300   66554 Third Street

Orange Adult School
555-9134   46589 Fourth Street

Public Library
555-0507   34661 Loro Road

Public Pool
555-4499   56321 Third Street

Senior Center
555-7342   97685 Sixth Street

Skate Park
555-6482   35211 Fourth Street

Superior Court
555-1796   96345 Orange Avenue

Village Elementary School
555-8462   34660 Loro Road

B. SUMMARIZE Listen to the phone conversations. Who did each person call? What information did he or she want?

1. Place: _Bay Books_

   Information: _store hours_

2. Place: _____

   Information: _____

3. Place: _____

   Information: _____

4. Place: _____

   Information: _____

5. Place: _____

   Information: _____

C. PLAN Sometimes it is helpful to write down what you want to say before you make a phone call. For each of the examples above, write what you might say when the person answers the phone.

1. _Hi. Could you please tell me what your store hours are?_

2. _____

3. _____

4. _____

5. _____

D. Using the questions you wrote above, practice short conversations with a partner. Change the underlined information for each item you wrote in Exercise C. Take turns being the clerk who answers the phone.

Clerk: Thank you for calling <u>Bay Books</u>. How can I help you?

You: <u>Hi. Could you please tell me what your store hours are?</u>

🎧 **E.** **Read and listen to the conversation.**

CD 1
TR 18

Host: Thank you for calling Scott's Steakhouse. How can I help you?

Caller: Yes, I was wondering if you are open for lunch.

Host: Yes, we are open for lunch from 11 a.m. to 3 p.m., Monday through Friday.

Caller: Do I need reservations?

Host: Reservations are not necessary, but we recommend them during the busy lunch hours.

Caller: Great. Thanks for your help!

Host: You're welcome. Goodbye.

Caller: Bye.

F. **Practice the conversation in Exercise E with a partner.**

> **SPEAK CLEARLY**
>
> When you are talking on the telephone, it is important that you pronounce every word very clearly (enunciate) and speak with rising and falling intonation. This is important because the person on the other end of the line can't see your mouth or your facial expressions.

G. **DEMONSTRATE Walk around the classroom and talk to four different classmates. Using the information below, have conversations like the one in Exercise E.**

Calling	Information needed	Response
Paris French Bistro	if reservations are needed and if there is a dress code	yes yes—coat and tie for men; no jeans for women
Loronado High School	location of the school's talent show	Coast Community Church at 11341 Fifth Street
Community Center	days and times of concerts in the park	every Sunday from 1 to 4 p.m.
Loronado Public Library	age required to get a library card	age five with parent's signature

LESSON 3 Why don't we . . . ?

GOAL ■ Give suggestions

A. Look at the picture. Where are Consuela and her husband Ricardo? Why are they talking to their neighbors? Read their conversation.

Ricardo: Let's find a good Italian restaurant. Can you think of where we could go?

Jim: Why don't we try this great little place called Island Pasta? It's a local hangout and I've heard the food is great!

Marie: I think they're closed tonight. How about going to Laredo's for a Mexican meal instead?

Consuela: Great idea!

Making suggestions	Responding to suggestions
Why don't we . . . ? We could . . . How about . . . ? Do you want to . . . ? Let's . . .	Great idea! Yes, let's do that! Sure! How about . . . instead?

B. SUGGEST With a partner, make new conversations. Use the topics below and suggestions from the chart. Talk about places in your community.

1. a good shoe store

2. a good movie for kids

3. a nice restaurant for your best friend's birthday dinner

4. a bookstore with a large selection of books

5. a good place to find really fresh fruit and vegetables

6. a place to eat Mexican food

7. a place to listen to good music

8. a bookstore to buy the required book for class

C. EVALUATE Read the notices on the community bulletin board. Which notice is the most interesting to you? Why?

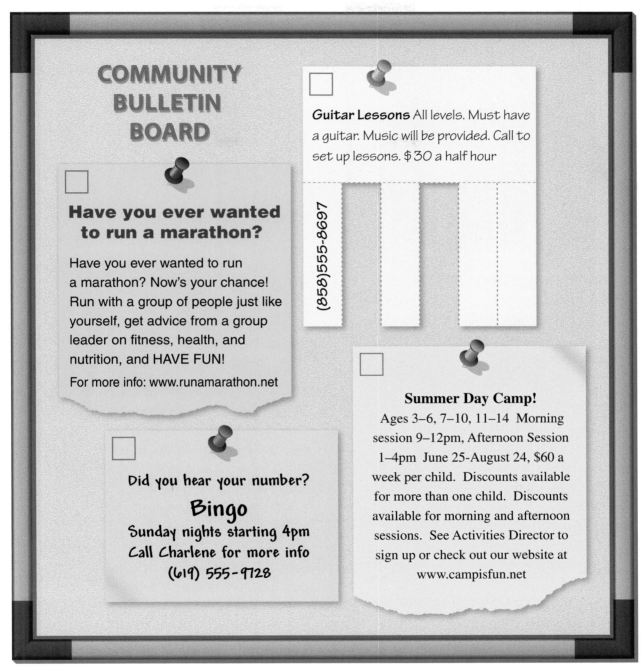

D. Listen to the community members. Where can they find the information they need? Write the correct number next to each notice above and on the notices on page 94.

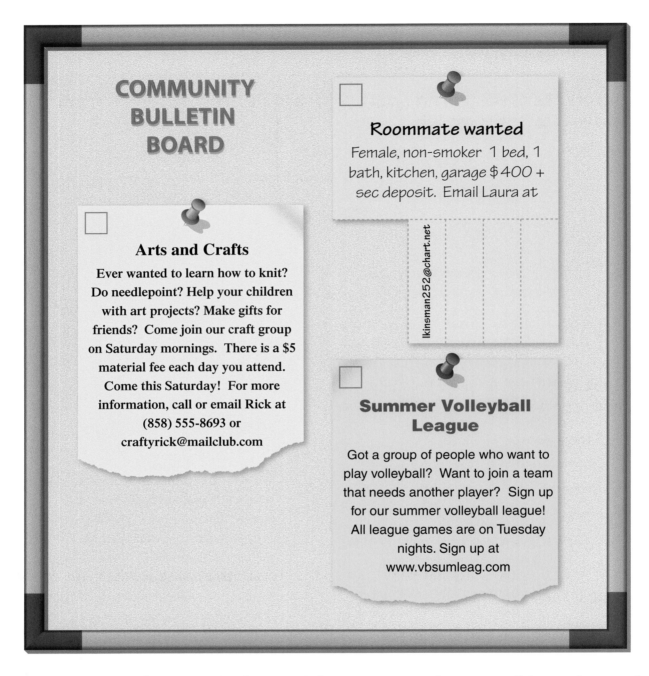

COMMUNITY BULLETIN BOARD

Roommate wanted
Female, non-smoker 1 bed, 1 bath, kitchen, garage $400 + sec deposit. Email Laura at

lkinsman252@chart.net

Arts and Crafts
Ever wanted to learn how to knit? Do needlepoint? Help your children with art projects? Make gifts for friends? Come join our craft group on Saturday mornings. There is a $5 material fee each day you attend. Come this Saturday! For more information, call or email Rick at (858) 555-8693 or craftyrick@mailclub.com

Summer Volleyball League
Got a group of people who want to play volleyball? Want to join a team that needs another player? Sign up for our summer volleyball league! All league games are on Tuesday nights. Sign up at www.vbsumleag.com

E. SUGGEST Work in pairs. Student A: Make a statement about one of the notices on the community bulletin board above and on page 93. Student B: Respond with a suggestion.

Student A: I need a place to send my kids for the summer while I'm at work.
Student B: Why don't you phone the Summer Day Camp?
Student A: That's a good idea.

F. CREATE Make a community bulletin board in your classroom. Think of things you could offer and make flyers. Share your ideas and make suggestions.

LESSON ④ How far is it?

GOAL ■ Interpret a road map

A. A legend helps you read the symbols on a road map. Write the correct words from the box next to the symbols.

✈ _____	3 _____
🚑 _____	5 _____
⛺ _____	8 _____
🏃 _____	🛏 _____
5 _____	🧺 _____

airport

hospital

campground

exit

freeway

interstate

state highway

state scenic highway

hotel/motel

rest area

B. Look at the map on page 96 and answer these questions with a partner.

1. Is there a hospital in Rose?

2. What interstate has rest areas?

3. Where is the nearest campground to Grandville?

4. Which highways are scenic?

5. Is there an airport near Lake Ellie?

C. **ESTIMATE** Look at the highway map scale and estimate the road distances on the map on page 96.

1. How far is it from Grandville to Rose?

2. How far is it from Poppington to Lake Ellie?

3. How far is it from Loronado to Poppington?

4. How far is it from Lake Ellie to Rose?

5. How far is it from Grandville to Poppington?

6. How far is it from Rose to Loronado?

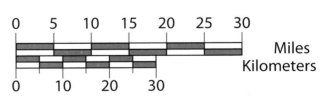

🎧 **D.** **Listen to the people giving directions. Where will the driver end up? Check (✓) the correct answer.**

CD 1
TR 20

1. ☐ Grandville   ☐ Rose   ☐ Lake Ellie   ☐ Loronado   ☐ Poppington

2. ☐ Grandville   ☐ Rose   ☐ Lake Ellie   ☐ Loronado   ☐ Poppington

3. ☐ Grandville   ☐ Rose   ☐ Lake Ellie   ☐ Loronado   ☐ Poppington

4. ☐ Grandville   ☐ Rose   ☐ Lake Ellie   ☐ Loronado   ☐ Poppington

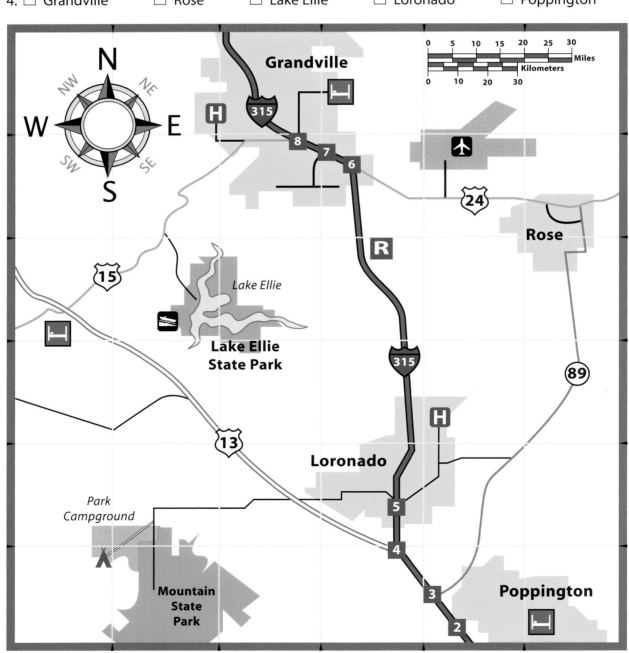

Conversation Strategy: Repeat for Clarification

When you are getting important information from someone, such as directions, it is always a good idea to ask for clarification. Asking for clarification means repeating back what was said or asking the other person to repeat it so you can double-check what you wrote down. One way to do this is to repeat just the part of the sentence that you are unsure of.

Examples: **A:** Take the highway exit and turn left.
                B: Turn left?
                A: Yes.

                A: Take 605 to 405 to 22.
                B: Did you say 605 to 405 to 22?
                A: Yes.

E. **EXPLAIN AND CLARIFY** Now, practice giving and receiving directions with a partner. Student A: Look at the map on page 96 to give directions. Student B: Write down what your partner says. If you get confused, ask your partner to slow down or repeat for clarification. Then, change roles.

EXAMPLE: From Rose to Grandville

Student A:	I live in Rose and I need to get to Grandville. What's the best way to get there?
Student B:	Take 24 West to 315 North. Follow 315 North to Exit 8.
Student A:	About how far is it?
Student B:	Sixty miles.
Student A:	Thank you so much.

1. Poppington to Lake Ellie

2. Loronado to Poppington

3. Lake Ellie to Rose

4. Rose to Loronado

5. Grandville to Poppington

F. **COMPARE** Now, look at the directions you wrote down when you were Student B. Compare them to the map. Are they correct?

LESSON **5** Volunteering

GOAL ■ Identify ways to volunteer in the community

A. **What is a volunteer? Make a list of three ways you can volunteer in your community.**

1. _____

2. _____

3. _____

B. **Look at the pictures. Where do you think these people are volunteering? Write your ideas on the line beneath each picture.**

1.

_____

2.

_____

3.

_____

4.

_____

5.

_____

6.

_____

7.

_____

8.

_____

9.

_____

C. REFLECT Before you volunteer, you need to think about what you would like to do or what you are good at. Look at the list below and check (✓) the things that you like to do and are good at. Add your own ideas to the bottom of the list.

Skills	I can . . .	I like to . . .	My partner can . . .	My partner likes to . . .
raise money for a cause				
build structures				
clean				
cook				
give a speech				
keep track of money				
make decorations				
make phone calls				
organize				
plan a meeting				
plan a party				
put books in alphabetical order				
spend time with children				
talk to people				
teach someone English				
teach someone to read				
teach someone math				
use a computer				

D. Now, interview a partner. Ask him or her what he or she likes to do and put checkmarks (✓) in the appropriate columns. Use these question beginnings: *Can you . . . ? Do you like to . . . ?*

E. What are some places in your community you might be able to volunteer? With a group, make a list. Share your list with the class.

		Places to Volunteer

F. **SUGGEST** Practice the conversation. Make new conversations. Give your partner an idea of places to volunteer based on the checklist.

Student A: I see you like to work with children. How about volunteering at the library for story time?

Student B: That's a great idea!

G. Select one of the places your partner suggested you volunteer and come up with questions you can ask when you call or visit the location.

1. _____

2. _____

3. _____

H. Now, practice asking your questions to a partner. Imagine that your partner works at the place where you want to volunteer. Your partner will have to be creative and come up with answers to your questions.

I. Find two places you can volunteer in your community and share with the class.

LIFESKILLS Everybody needs to get involved

Before You Watch

A. **Look at the picture. Complete each sentence.**

1. Mrs. Sanchez leads a(n)

   _____.

2. Naomi and Hector are helping to

   _____ clothes for
   a local shelter.

3. A shelter is a _____.

While You Watch

B. ▶ **Watch the video. Complete the dialog.**

Naomi:	I'm fine, thank you Mrs. Sanchez. I brought in a few things for your clothing (1) _____drive_____.
Mrs. Sanchez:	Thank you so much.
Naomi:	I have a lot of (2) _____ clothes. It's the least I could do.
Mrs. Sanchez:	That's so nice of you, Naomi. I know somebody will really (3) _____ these clothes.
Naomi:	Could I help you with anything? I'm not working today and I don't have any classes. Do you need any (4) _____?
Mrs. Sanchez:	I could use your help. Let me see … Would you mind helping me (5) _____ the clothing?

Check Your Understanding

C. **Make the questions more polite. Use the words in parentheses.**

1. Where is Orange Avenue? (Can you show me) _Can you show me where Orange Avenue is?_

2. Are there any shelters downtown? (Do you know if) _____

3. When does the shelter open? (Can you tell me) _____

4. What do volunteers do? (Can you explain) _____

5. How can I get public assistance? (Would you mind telling me) _____

Review

A. In your community, where would you go to do the following things? Write one idea on each line.

1. get a bus schedule _____

2. borrow books _____

3. get a flu vaccine _____

4. take an art class _____

5. use a computer _____

B. Change the questions below to embedded questions.

1. What is the address of the library?

   _____

2. Do you sell vitamins?

   _____

3. What time does the museum close?

   _____

4. Is the Adult School on this street?

   _____

5. When do classes begin?

   _____

C. Imagine you are calling the places that you wrote down in Exercise A. With a partner, practice having telephone conversations about each of the topics listed.

Get a bus schedule

Receptionist: Transit Authority, can I help you?

Caller: Yes, I was wondering how I can get a bus schedule.

Receptionist: Well, you can come down to our office and pick one up or you can go online and print out a schedule of any route you want.

Caller: Really? Oh, that's a great idea. I'll use my computer to print out a schedule. Thanks!

Receptionist: You're welcome.

D. Imagine that you just moved into your neighborhood. Write four questions you might ask your new neighbors about different places to go. Then, practice asking and answering the questions with a partner. Write the suggestions that your partner gives you in the chart below.

Questions	Suggestions
1. Do you know of a good coffee shop?	1. Why don't you try the Happy Kettle on 4th Street?
2.	2.
3.	3.
4.	4.
5.	5.

E. Now, ask your partner to give you directions from your current location to the four places he or she suggested. Write down the directions. Ask for clarification to double-check them with your partner.

1. _____

2. _____

3. _____

4. _____

F. Read the map and answer the questions.

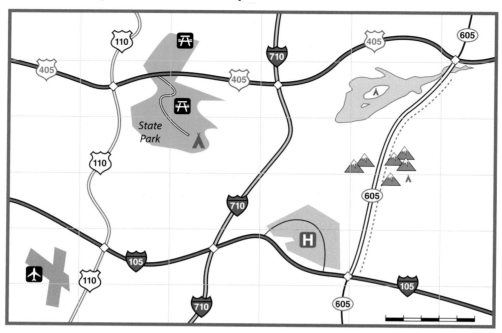

1. What highway would you take to get to the hospital? _____

2. What highway would you take to get to the state park? _____

3. Which highways run north-south? _____

4. How would you get from the lake to the hospital? _____

_____

G. List three things you like to do. For each thing you like to do, write two places where you could volunteer.

Things that I like to do	Places where I could volunteer
1.	1. 2.
2.	1. 2.
3.	1. 2.

H. Take out the dictionary you started in Unit 2. Brainstorm five new words you learned in this unit. If you don't remember the meanings, look them up in a dictionary.

✓ **Create a community resource guide**

With a team, you will create a community resource guide. This project can be done in two ways:

a. Each team creates its own guide.

b. Each team creates a portion of a guide and all parts are combined at the end to make a class guide.

1. **COLLABORATE** Form a team with four or five students. Choose roles for each member of your team.

Position	Job description	Student name
Student 1: Team Leader	Check that everyone speaks English and participates.	
Student 2: Writer	Take notes and write information for guide.	
Student 3: Designer	Design and add art to guide.	
Students 4/5: Spokespeople	Report information to the class. Prepare team for the presentation.	

2. As a class, decide what information should go in your guide(s), such as the names of local services, medical facilities, restaurants, events, and places to volunteer. Make a list on the board.

3. Decide if each team will create its own guide or if each team will work on a portion of a class guide. (If the second option is chosen, decide what section each team will work on.)

4. Create your guide or portion of the class guide. Each portion should include addresses, phone numbers, basic information, and a map. (Use the phone book or the Internet if you need to.)

5. Put your guide together.

6. Present your guide or portion of your guide to the class.

EXPLORER REBECCA SKINNER

Giving Personal Stories a Voice

"I am passionate about giving a voice to people who feel they cannot be heard."
—Rebecca Skinner

A. **ANALYZE** Rebecca's uncle once said to her, "You cannot lower the mountain, therefore, you must elevate yourself."

What does this quote mean to you?

_____

_____

_____

B. Do you remember the following disasters? Interpret the chart with a partner.

Name	Place	Disaster	Year(s)	Casualties	
Hurricane Katrina	New Orleans	hurricane	2005	1,833	costliest natural disaster, one of the 5 deadliest hurricanes in the history of the US
Indian Ocean Earthquake and Tsunami	Indonesia Sri Lanka India Thailand	earthquake + tsunami	2004	about 228,000	largest magnitude earthquake in 40 years

C. Rebecca Skinner is a photographer from Denver, Colorado. Read the interview with her below.

What did you want to be when you were growing up?

I grew up always knowing that I wanted to explore.

How did you get started in your field of work?

In the fall of 2010, I won a grant from my university to travel to New Orleans to photograph the five-year difference from Hurricane Katrina. That trip was really life-changing, and it made me realize that photography is something I would like to do for the rest of my life.

What inspires you to dedicate your life to photography?

Studying social work made me passionate about giving a voice to people who feel they cannot be heard. Through both my tsunami and Hurricane Katrina photo projects, I've realized that post-natural disaster communities are often forgotten about. I strongly believe that how a community recovers (or not) is just as important as the disaster itself. Photographically documenting these communities gives personal stories a voice.

Do you have a hero?

My uncle, Todd Skinner, who was a professional rock climber. He always encouraged us to push our own limits, to explore wild places, and to be a storyteller. He once said, "You cannot lower the mountain, therefore, you must elevate yourself." Also, I have the most incredible parents in the world.

What has been your favorite experience in the field?

My favorite field experience was getting to fly a kite in the middle of a rice paddy with all the villagers we had lived with in Sumatra. The sun was setting, everyone was laughing, and trying to communicate though we were speaking two different languages. It was like something I've dreamed or read about.

D. With a small group, discuss the following questions.

1. Rebecca photographs communities that have gone through disasters. In what way do her photographs help these communities?

2. Her uncle Todd encouraged her to be a storyteller. Do you think she is? Explain why.

3. If you were going to help a community that had gone through a disaster, what could you do?

E. Choose one of the topics above and write a paragraph.

Solar-Powered Water Heaters and the Symbolic Nature of Communication

Before You Watch

A. The sun does many important things. Circle the things you already know. Share your answers with a partner and discuss.

makes energy	gives us light	helps plants grow
warms the earth	makes rain	makes wind

B. Look at the world map. Do you have a lot of sunshine where you live? What places have the most sunshine? The least? Discuss as a class.

World Sunshine Map

Average yearly total number of house of Bright Sunshine.

Over 3000	2000 – 3000	2000 – 1000	1000 – 500	Under 500

C. Read the words and definitions. Then, complete each sentence.

> I think we get 1,000 – 2,000 hours of sunshine per year in New York City. That's a lot. Some places in Europe get under 500 hours a year.

recycle	to use something again instead of throwing it away
solar power	energy we use that comes directly from the sun
sanitation	making something free from dirt and disease by removing waste and trash
solar panels	a device that uses direct sunlight to heat water or to make electricity
renewable energy	energy that comes from natural resources such as sunlight, wind, and rain; it can not be used up

1. I _____ clothes all the time. I often buy used T-shirts and jeans online.

2. The boat uses its sails and the wind to move. It uses a type of _____.

3. The water heater uses _____. We don't need gas or electricity beause the sun heats our water.

4. The _____ in the city is not very good. You should be careful about drinking the water.

5. Areceli's house has _____ on the roof. This device uses the sunlight to give her electricity.

D. Discuss what the expression "One man's garbage is another man's treasure." means to you.

> People can reuse what others throw away.

E. **Watch the video. Then, complete each sentence with the correct word.**

rooftops	city	trash	sunshine	garbage

1. Cairo, Egypt has a lot of _____.

2. Cairo is a big _____ with many different people.

3. There is a lot of _____ on their rooftops, too.

4. Egyptians save their _____ to reuse in the future.

5. Egyptians use their _____ for water tanks, satellite dishes, and animals.

F. **Watch the video again. Listen and match the words with the descriptions.**

1. _____ chaos

2. _____ the sun

3. _____ solar heater

4. _____ T.H. Culhane

5. _____ "going green"

a. it uses sunshine for fuel

b. National Geographic Explorer

c. Egypt's greatest natural resource

d. Cairo recycles or reuses its garbage

e. rooftops with garbage and animals

G. **Watch the video again. Which statements about the solar water heaters are true? Circle the correct answers.**

1. Solar water heaters are very expensive.

2. Solar water heaters improve sanitation.

3. Solar water heaters can make cold water, too.

4. Solar water heaters use solar panels.

5. Solar water heaters need electricity to work.

6. We can use garbage to make solar water heaters.

After You Watch

H. In what ways do you use hot water in your home? Make a list and share it with a partner.

washing clothes
_____   _____
_____   _____
_____   _____

I. What is there in your garbage that you can recycle? Make a list and discuss as a class.

cans
_____   _____
_____   _____
_____   _____

J. Categorize. Write the descriptions in the correct columns in your notebooks.

saves money	expensive	recyclable materials	needs sunlight
small carbon footprint	needs electricity	less pollution	renewable energy
large carbon footprint			

Solar water heater	Electric water heater

K. How can you use solar power in your home? Brainstorm in small groups. Then, discuss as a class.

Health

Using special techniques, a photographer captures a sneeze as it happens.

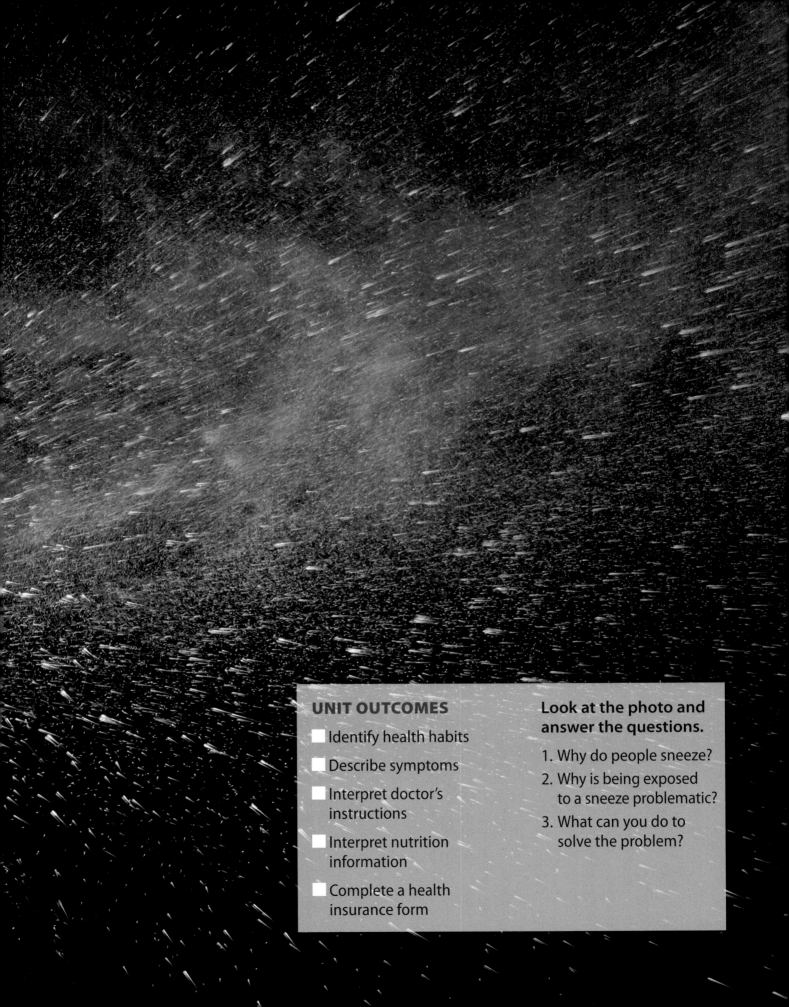

UNIT OUTCOMES

☐ Identify health habits

☐ Describe symptoms

☐ Interpret doctor's instructions

☐ Interpret nutrition information

☐ Complete a health insurance form

Look at the photo and answer the questions.

1. Why do people sneeze?

2. Why is being exposed to a sneeze problematic?

3. What can you do to solve the problem?

LESSON **1** Health habits

GOAL ◼ Identify health habits

A. **What are these people doing? Which activities are healthy? Which activities are unhealthy? Make two lists below.**

Healthy Habits	Unhealthy Habits

B. **Can you think of other healthy and unhealthy habits? Add them to your lists.**

C. CLASSIFY Look at each health habit in the chart below and decide if it is healthy or unhealthy. Put a check (✓) in the correct column.

Health habit	Healthy	Unhealthy
watching a lot of TV		
doing puzzles		
drinking too much alcohol		
drinking water		
eating fruits and vegetables		
eating junk food		
lifting weights		
meditating		
playing sports		
reading		
sleeping		
smoking		
spending time with friends and family		
taking illegal drugs		
walking		

D. There are two different types of health—mental health and physical health. Mental health is anything related to your mind and psychological well-being. Physical health is anything related to your body, both fitness and nutrition.

Look at the health habits you checked as healthy in the chart above. Decide which type of health each one benefits and write it in the correct column in the chart below.

Mental health	Physical health
doing puzzles	

E.   INTERPRET Ms. Tracy's students took a poll to find out what bad health habits they have. Read the bar graph with their results and answer the questions.

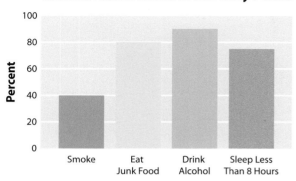

The Bad Health Habits of Ms. Tracy's Class

HOW TO CALCULATE PERCENTAGE

1. First, find out the total number of students in your class.

2. Then, divide the total number of students into the number of students who answered the question *yes*.

   EXAMPLE: In a class of 25 students, 15 students exercise.

$$25\overline{)15.00} = .60$$
$$\underline{15.00}$$
$$0$$

3. Move the decimal over two places to the right to get the percentage.

   .60 = 60%

1. What percentage of students eats junk food? _____

2. What percentage of students sleeps less than eight hours? _____

3. What percentage of students *doesn't* smoke? _____

4. What percentage of students *doesn't* drink alcohol? _____

5. What is the worst health habit Ms. Tracy's class has? _____

F.   GRAPH In a group, list four healthy habits. Take a poll in your class to see who practices these healthy habits. Make sure you ask everyone. Make a bar graph of your findings.

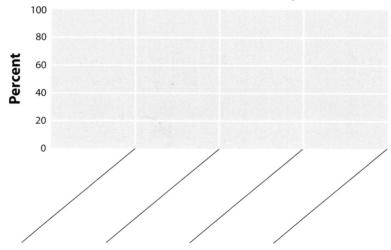

The Good Health Habits of My Class

LESSON ② What's the problem?

GOAL ▪ Describe symptoms

A. **PREDICT** Look at the picture. Who are the people in the picture? What are they saying? Then, read the conversation.

Doctor:	Hello, John. What seems to be the problem?
John:	<u>I've been coughing a lot</u>.
Doctor:	Anything else?
John:	Yes, <u>my chest has been hurting</u>, too.
Doctor:	It sounds like you might have <u>bronchitis</u>. I'd like to do some tests to be sure, and then I'll give you a prescription to relieve your symptoms.
John:	Thanks, Doc.

B. Practice the conversation with a partner. Then, practice the conversation several more times, replacing the underlined parts with the information below.

Symptom 1	Symptom 2	Diagnosis
1. I've been blowing my nose a lot.	My body has been aching.	common cold
2. My leg's been hurting.	I haven't been walking properly.	muscle spasm
3. I've been throwing up.	I've been feeling faint and dizzy.	flu

C. Study the chart with your teacher.

Present Perfect Continuous	
Example	**Form**
I *have been resting* for three hours.	Affirmative sentence: *has/have + been* + present participle
He *hasn't been sleeping* well recently.	Negative sentence: *has/have + not + been* + present participle
How long *have they lived/have they been living* here?	Question: *has/have* + subject + *been* + present participle

- To emphasize the duration of an activity or to state that it started in the past and continues in the present. Example: The president *has been sleeping* since 9 a.m.
- To show that an activity has been in progress recently. Example: You*'ve been going* to the doctor a lot lately.
- With some verbs (*work, live, teach*), there is no difference in meaning between the present perfect and the present perfect continuous. Example: They *have lived/have been living* here since 2010.

Note: Some verbs are not usually used in the continuous form. These include *be, believe, hate, have, know, like,* and *want*.

D. Complete the sentences using the present perfect continuous form of the verbs in parentheses and suitable time expressions.

TIME	
for + period of time	*since* + point in time
two weeks	Tuesday
five days	5:30 p.m.
a month	1964
a long time	last night
a while	I was a child

1. We __have been going__ (go) to our

   family doctor for __a long time__ .

2. The kids _____ (sleep) since _____ .

3. The couple _____ (practice) medicine in

   Mexico for _____ .

4. I _____ (work) at the same job for _____ .

5. How long _____ (you, study) to be an optometrist?

6. Satomi _____ (not / feel well) since _____ .

7. The boy _____ (cough) since _____ .

8. Enrico _____ (take) his medicine for _____ .

9. Minh _____ (think) about changing jobs for _____ .

10. They _____ (go) to the gym together for _____ .

E. Now, review the present perfect with your teacher.

Present Perfect	
Example	**Form**
He *has seen* the doctor. I *have moved* four times in my life.	Affirmative sentence: *has/have* + past participle
They *haven't been* to the hospital to see her.	Negative sentence: *has/have* + *not* + past participle OR *has/have* + *never* + past participle
Have you *written* to your mother?	Question: *has/have* + subject + past participle

- When something happened (or didn't happen) at an unspecified time in the past. Example: She *has* never *broken* her arm.
- When something happened more than once in the past (and could possibly happen again in the future). Example: I *have moved* four times in my life.
- When something started at a specific time in the past and continues in the present. Example: They *have lived* here for ten years.

F. Write the present perfect or the present perfect continuous form of the verbs in parentheses. In some sentences, you will also need to decide if *for* or *since* should be used.

1. They _____ (be) to their new doctor several times.

2. Marco _____ (have) asthma _____ 1995.

3. She _____ (give) me a lot of help _____ I moved here.

4. I _____ (not / see) the dentist _____ a year.

5. _____ (you / see) the new hospital downtown?

6. _____ (you / wait) _____ a long time?

7. Santiago _____ (miss) two appointments this week.

8. We _____ (cook) _____ three hours.

9. He _____ (not / examine) her _____ she was a child.

10. How long _____ (you / know) Maria?

G. DEMONSTRATE Work in groups of three or four. Ask and answer questions beginning with *How long*. Use the present perfect or present perfect continuous.

EXAMPLE: How long have you been going to the same doctor?
How long have you had a headache?

GOAL ■ Interpret doctor's instructions

🎧 **A.** **PUT IN ORDER** Look at the picture. What are the people talking about? What do you think they are saying? Listen and number the things the doctor told Rosa about her health in the correct order (1–5).

_____ "I can give you some more tests."

_____ "The most important thing is to stay active."

_____ "You'll have to come back in two weeks."

_____ "If you start exercising more, your cholesterol level should go down."

_____ "If you don't stop eating junk food, you will have serious health problems."

🎧 **B.** Now, listen to Rosa reporting her conversation to her friend. Fill in the missing words.

1. She said she ____would____ give ____me____ some more tests.

2. The doctor told me the most important thing _____ to stay active.

3. She told me if _____ _____ exercising more, _____ cholesterol should go down.

4. She said if _____ _____ stop eating junk food, _____ _____ have serious health problems.

5. She said _____ _____ to come back in two weeks.

C. What differences do you notice between the sentences in Exercise A and Exercise B? Study the chart with your teacher.

Direct Speech	Indirect Speech	Rule
"You have to exercise more."	The doctor _explained_ (that) _I had_ to exercise more.	• Change pronoun. • Change present tense to past tense.
"The most important thing is your health."	The doctor _said_ (that) the most important thing _was_ my health.	

D. **Match the kinds of doctors with the type of treatment they provide.**

| obstetrician | podiatrist | chiropractor | dentist | pediatrician |

_____ _____ _____

_____ _____

E. **RESTATE** **Read the statements and decide what kind of doctor said each one. Use indirect speech to tell your partner what each person said.**

"Your child is in perfect health!"

The pediatrician said my child was in perfect health.

INDIRECT SPEECH VERBS

announced	stated
answered	said
complained	explained
replied	agreed

1. "You need to brush your gums and floss your teeth every day."

2. "Your children are eating too many sweets and sugary foods. They need to eat more fruits and vegetables."

3. "It is a good idea to go to prenatal classes for at least three weeks."

4. "The shoes you are wearing aren't good for your feet."

5. "You'll hurt your back if you don't bend your knees to lift heavy objects."

6. "You need to make an appointment to have those cavities filled."

7. "You need to make sure you take your vitamins every day."

F. Study the chart.

Direct Speech	Indirect Speech
I want to lose weight. Your test results are negative.	I told *you* (that) I wanted to lose weight. He told *me* (that) my test results were negative.
It is important to check your heart rate. I feel sick.	My personal trainer said (that) it was important to check my heart rate. She complained (that) she felt sick.

- Some verbs are usually followed by an indirect object or pronoun. (*tell, assure, advise, convince, notify, promise, remind, teach, warn*)
- Some verbs are not followed by an indirect object or pronoun. (*say, agree, announce, answer, complain, explain, reply, state*)

G. Rewrite each quote using indirect speech with the subject and verb in parentheses.

1. "You need to walk for 30 minutes every day." (the doctor, remind)

    The doctor reminded me that I needed to walk for 30 minutes every day.

2. "He needs to stop smoking." (the cardiologist, warn)

    _____

3. "You have a very balanced diet." (the nutritionist, assure)

    _____

4. "She is very healthy." (the pediatrician, agree)

    _____

5. "You eat too much junk food." (the doctor, convince)

    _____

6. "I read nutrition labels for every food I eat." (I, tell, the doctor)

    _____

7. "We want to start exercising together." (our parents, announce)

    _____

H. RETELL Think of a conversation you had with a doctor or health care professional. Tell your partner what the person said to you.

LESSON **4** Nutrition labels

GOAL ■ Interpret nutrition information

A. **Do you read the nutrition labels on the food that you buy? What do you look for? Why?**

B. **SCAN** **Scan the nutrition label and answer the questions.**

Nutrition Facts		
Serving Size 2 oz. (56gm)		
Servings Per Container 8		
Amount Per Serving		
Calories 200	Calories from Fat 10	
% Daily Value*		
Total Fat 1g		2%
Saturated Fat 0g		
Cholesterol 0mg		
Sodium 0mg		
Total Carbohydrate 42g		14%
Dietary Fiber 2g		8%
Sugars 1g		
Protein 7g		
Vitamin A		0%
Calcium		0%
Thiamin		35%
Niacin		15%
Vitamin C		0%
Iron		10%
Riboflavin		15%
Folate		30%

*Percent Davily Values are based on a 2,000-calorie diet. Your daily values may be higher or lower depending on your caloric needs:

Calories		2,000	2,500
Total Fat	Less than	65g	80g
Sat Fat	Less than	20g	25g
Cholesterol	Less than	300mg	300mg
Sodium	Less than	2,400mg	2,400mg
Total Carbohydrate		300g	375g
Dietary Fiber		25g	30g

Calories per gram:
Fat 9   Carbohydrate 4   Protein 4

Ingredients: Semolina, Niacin, Iron, Thiamin Mononitrate, Riboflavin, Folic Acid

1. How much protein is in one serving of this product? _____

2. How many calories are in one serving of this product? _____ How many

    of those calories are from fat? _____

3. What vitamins and/or minerals does this product contain per serving?

    _____   _____   _____   _____

    _____   _____   _____   _____

4. How many carbohydrates are in one serving of this product? _____

5. How much fat is in one serving of this product? _____ How much of the

    fat is saturated? _____

6. How much of this product is one serving? _____

7. How many servings are in the box? _____

C. MATCH These words can be found on a nutrition label. (See the highlighted words on the nutrition label on page 123.) Write the correct letter next to each definition. Use each letter only once.

a. saturated fat   b. sodium   c. calories

d. carbohydrates   e. serving size   f. protein

g. ingredients   h. cholesterol   i. vitamins

j. fiber

_____ 1. This is the amount of food that a person actually eats at one time.

_____ 2. This is the amount of energy supplied by a kind of food.

_____ 3. This is a type of fat. It can contribute to heart disease.

_____ 4. This ingredient of food is not digested, but it aids digestion.

_____ 5. This type of nutrient indicates the salt content of food.

_____ 6. This helps to build and repair muscles. It is found mainly in meat, fish, eggs, beans, and cheese.

_____ 7. These are whatever is contained in a type of food. On a nutrition label, they are presented in order of weight from most to least.

_____ 8. These are the best source of energy and can be found in breads, grains, fruits, and vegetables.

_____ 9. Eating too much of this can cause you to have heart disease and to be overweight.

_____ 10. These nutrients are found in food and help to keep your body healthy.

D. How much do you know about the nutrients on food labels? Discuss the questions below with a small group.

1. Why is it good to read nutrition labels?

2. What do complex carbohydrates do for your body?

3. What does saturated fat do to your body?

4. What type of person should watch his or her sodium intake?

5. How much protein should you eat per day?

6. Why are simple carbohydrates good?

7. Why is it good to eat fiber?

E. Read the information about food labels.

Reading Nutritional Information on Food Labels

Knowing how to read the food label on packaged foods can help you build better eating habits. Here's a rundown of the basics you'll find on a food label and how you can use the information to improve your daily diet:

1. Serving Size The serving size on the label is supposed to be close to a "real-life" serving size—no more listing a teaspoon of salad dressing when most of us use a tablespoon. The information on the rest of the label is based on data for one serving. Remember, a package may contain more than one serving.

2. Calories The number of calories tells you how many calories are in one serving. The number of calories from fat tells you how many of those calories come from fat. Try to find foods with low amounts of calories from fat.

3. Fat This is where you look if you are trying to count fat grams. Total fat is important to watch, but saturated fat is particularly bad for you. Saturated fat raises your blood cholesterol level, which could lead to heart trouble.

4. Cholesterol Along with the saturated-fat information above, cholesterol amounts are important for anyone concerned about heart disease. High levels of cholesterol can lead to serious heart problems later in life.

5. Sodium Sodium (or salt) levels are important to monitor if you have high blood pressure.

6. Carbohydrates These fit into two categories—complex carbohydrates (dietary fiber) and simple carbohydrates (sugars). You want to eat more complex carbohydrates and fewer simple carbohydrates. Diets high in complex carbohydrates have been shown to fight cancer and heart disease. Simple carbohydrates are good for energy, but if you eat too many of them, you can expect your waistline to grow.

7. Fiber Fiber consists of complex carbohydrates that cannot be absorbed by the body. It aids digestion and can help lower blood cholesterol. High fiber foods include fruits, vegetables, brown rice, and whole-grain products.

8. Protein The food label doesn't specify a daily percentage or guideline for protein consumption because so much depends on individual needs. An athlete needs more than an office worker, but in a typical 2,000-calorie diet, most people need no more than 50 grams of protein per day.

9. Vitamins and Minerals The FDA requires only Vitamin A, Vitamin C, iron, and calcium amounts to be on food labels although food companies can voluntarily list others. Try to get 100% of each of these essential vitamins and minerals every day.

10. Ingredients Ingredients are listed on food labels by weight from the most to the least. This section can alert you to any ingredients you may want to avoid because of food allergies.

F. **DEMONSTRATE** How much do you know about nutrition now? Check (✓) *True* or *False* for each statement.

	True	False
1. Reading food labels can improve your eating habits.	☐	☐
2. Diets high in complex carbohydrates can help fight cancer and heart disease.	☐	☐
3. Saturated fat lowers your blood cholesterol level.	☐	☐
4. You should watch your sodium intake if you have high blood pressure.	☐	☐
5. Most people need at least 100 grams of protein per day.	☐	☐
6. Simple carbohydrates are good for energy.	☐	☐
7. Foods with fiber can help lower cholesterol.	☐	☐

LESSON 5 Do you want dental coverage?

GOAL ■ Complete a health insurance form

A. If you were looking for a good health insurance company, what things would you look for? Check (✓) the items below that would be most important for you. Share your answers with the class.

☐ dental coverage ☐ low deductible

☐ prescription plan ☐ low co-pay

☐ vision plan ☐ good choice of providers

☐ low premium ☐ good reputation

B. Most insurance companies offer two types of coverage—HMO and PPO. What do these two terms stand for?

HMO: _____ _____ _____

PPO: _____ _____ _____

C. **CLASSIFY** What are the differences between an *HMO* and *PPO*? Work with a small group and write *HMO* or *PPO* on the line before each statement.

1. _____ higher out-of-pocket expenses

2. _____ low or sometimes free co-pay

3. _____ you can see any doctor you want to at any time

4. _____ you must choose one primary-care physician

5. _____ higher monthly premium

6. _____ lower monthly premium

7. _____ you must get a referral from your primary-care physician to see another doctor

8. _____ low or sometimes no out-of-pocket expenses

D. Skim the health insurance application on this page and the next page. Put a check (✓) next to every part you can answer. Underline the parts you are not sure about.

Employee Applicant Information

First Name: _____ Middle Name: _____ Last Name: _____

Home Address:

Street: _____ City: _____ State: _____ Zip Code: _____

Sex: Male Female

Social Security Number: _____-_____-_____

Date of Birth: (mm / dd / yyyy) ____ / _____ / _____

Marital Status: ____ Married ____ Single

Work Phone: (_____) _____-_____ Home Phone: (_____) _____-_____

Cell Phone: (_____) _____-_____ E-mail: _____

Job Title: _____

Hours Worked Per Week: _____

Annual Salary: _____

Tobacco: Have you or your spouse used any tobacco products in the past 12 months?

        Employee: ____Yes ____No   Spouse: ____Yes ____No

Dental: Do you want dental coverage? ____Yes ____No

Prescription Card: Do you want a prescription card? ____Yes ____No

Dependents: Dependents you want covered on this policy.

Spouse: _____

Date of Birth: (mm / dd / yyyy) _____ / _____ / _____ Sex: ____Male ____Female

Child #1: _____

Date of Birth: (mm / dd / yyyy) _____ / _____ / _____ Sex: ____Male ____Female

Child #2: _____

Date of Birth: (mm / dd / yyyy) _____ / _____ / _____ Sex: ____Male ____Female

A-1: Within the last four (4) years, have you or any dependant received or been recommended to have treatment for any disorders or conditions of the following? Please check all that apply.

❑ Back ❑ Stroke ❑ Intestinal ❑ Colon ❑ Kidney ❑ Muscular ❑ Heart or Circulatory

❑ Cancer ❑ Diabetes ❑ Respiratory ❑ Mental or Emotional ❑ Liver

A-2: Within the last four (4) years, have you or any dependent used drugs not prescribed by a physician, been advised to have treatment or been treated for drug abuse, alcoholism, or been a member of Alcoholics Anonymous? Yes   No

A-3: Have you or any dependant ever had a positive blood test indicating HIV antibodies or been treated and/ or advised by a medical practitioner as having Acquired Immune Deficiency Syndrome (AIDS), AIDS Related Complex (ARC), or any other immune system deficiency? Yes   No

A-4: Have you or any dependent been hospitalized, had surgery, or had more than $5,000 in medical expenses in the last twelve (12) months? _____ Yes _____ No

A-5: Are you or any dependent pregnant? _____ Yes _____ No

   If "Yes," what is your estimated due date? _____

A-6: Within the last four (4) years, have you or any dependent received or been recommended to have treatment for any disorders or conditions of the following? Please check all that apply.

❑ Ear ❑ Hernia ❑ Thyroid ❑ Breast

❑ Eye ❑ Allergy ❑ Digestive System

❑ Joint ❑ Asthma ❑ Reproductive Organs

❑ Ulcer ❑ Arthritis ❑ High Blood Pressure

A-7: Within the last four (4) years, have you or any dependent received treatment or been advised to seek treatment for any reason not already mentioned? _____ Yes _____ No

Employee Name: _____

Date: (mm/dd/yyyy) _____ / _____ / _____

E. Work in pairs. Use a dictionary to help you understand the parts of the form that you underlined.

F. DETERMINE Work with a small group to answer the following questions.

   1. Why do you think health insurance companies need all of this information?

   2. Why is it important to have health insurance?

G. Now that you understand all the parts of the application, fill it out.

   Note: If any information is too personal, just think about the answer and don't write it in your book.

LIFESKILLS ▶ Thanks for the advice, doctor

Before You Watch

A. **Look at the picture. Complete each sentence.**

1. Mrs. Sanchez is in a

   _____ office.

2. Mrs. Sanchez is having a

   _____ exam.

3. Dr. Badaoui is writing a

   _____ for Mrs. Sanchez.

While You Watch

B. ▶ **Watch the video. Complete the dialog.**

Mrs. Sanchez:	Yes. First, we looked at the results of my (1) ___*blood test*___. You said that my cholesterol count was very high. Then, you recommended another test. Are those the results?
Dr. Badaoui:	Yes, they are. The results show that your (2) _____ count is still very high. Tell me, have you made any changes to your diet since your last appointment?
Mrs. Sanchez:	Oh, yes. I've changed my diet quite a bit. I've stopped eating (3) _____, and I don't eat as many dairy products, either.
Dr. Badaoui:	And have you been getting any (4) _____?
Mrs. Sanchez:	Yes, I've been (5) _____ every day, and I love it.
Dr. Badaoui:	That's good. It sounds like you've been making some healthy changes in your (6) _____.

Check Your Understanding

C. **Read the statements. Write T for *True* or F for *False*.**

1. Mrs. Sanchez's cholesterol count is low.   ___F___

2. She is now eating less red meat but more dairy products.   _____

3. She runs every day.   _____

4. The doctor wants her to take one pill a day.   _____

5. The doctor wants her to come back in three weeks.   _____

Review

Learner Log

I can identify good and bad health habits.
☐ Yes ☐ Maybe ☐ No

I can describe symptoms to a doctor.
☐ Yes ☐ Maybe ☐ No

A. In your opinion, what are the three most important good health habits to have?

1. _____

2. _____

3. _____

B. In your opinion, what are the three worst health habits to have?

1. _____

2. _____

3. _____

C. Complete the sentences using the present perfect simple or present perfect continuous form of the verb in parentheses.

1. I (not / eat) _____ meat for three years.

2. Sara (go) _____ to yoga classes since September.

3. Andres (drink) _____ two liters of water today.

4. I (not / sleep) _____ well recently.

5. I (never / smoke) _____ a cigarette.

6. Why (you / choose) _____ such a stressful job?

7. Marna (wheeze) _____ since last night.

8. We (see) _____ the same doctor for over ten years.

9. My father (have) _____ diabetes since he was a child.

10. The children (not / brush) _____ their teeth very well.

Learner Log

I can interpret doctor's instructions.	I can identify vitamins and nutritional content of foods.
▮ Yes ▮ Maybe ▮ No	▮ Yes ▮ Maybe ▮ No

D. Write the type of doctor you would see if you were having problems with the following.

1. feet _____

2. back _____

3. pregnancy _____

4. baby's ears _____

5. teeth _____

E. Change the sentences from direct speech to indirect speech.

1. "My daughter is sick."

Maria said that _____.

2. "We won't be able to come to the meeting."

Luis and Ricardo told me _____.

3. "They don't have time to go out."

Hanif said _____.

4. "You need to take the medicine on an empty stomach."

The doctor explained that _____.

5. "Your son is eating too much sugar."

The pediatrician said _____.

6. "My back has been hurting for two months."

I told the chiropractor _____.

7. "You need to take your prenatal vitamins every day."

The obstetrician told me _____.

8. "Your husband needs to stay off his feet for a few hours a day."

The podiatrist warned me _____.

F.   Match the descriptions to the nutrition items.

1. _____ calories
2. _____ carbohydrates
3. _____ cholesterol
4. _____ saturated fat
5. _____ fiber
6. _____ ingredients
7. _____ protein
8. _____ serving size
9. _____ sodium
10. _____ vitamins

a. listed on a food label by weight

b. complex carbohydrates that cannot be absorbed by the body

c. salt

d. dietary fiber and sugar

e. try to get 100% of each every day

f. energy supplied by food

g. a type of fat that can contribute to heart disease

h. the amount of food a person eats at one time

i. helps build and repair muscles

j. too much of this could lead to heart disease

G.   What is important to you when looking for health insurance? Make a list.

_____

_____

_____

_____

H.   Do you remember what you learned about word families in the Pre-Unit? If not, look back at page 9 in Lesson 3 of the Pre-Unit. Complete as much of the chart as you can with words from this unit. Then, complete the word families using your dictionary.

Noun	Verb	Adjective	Adverb
_____	advise	_____	_____
insurance	_____	_____	—
_____	—	habitual	_____
medicine	_____	_____	_____
_____	_____	_____	_____
_____	_____	_____	_____

Look in your dictionary and see if any new words you have written down have other "family members." Add them to your dictionary.

✓ # Create a community health pamphlet

With a team, you will create a pamphlet to distribute to the community about good health practices.

1. **COLLABORATE** Form a team with four or five students. Choose positions for each member of your team.

Position	Job description	Student name
Student 1: Team Leader	Check that everyone speaks English and participates.	
Student 2: Writer	Take notes and write information for pamphlet.	
Student 3: Designer	Design and add art to pamphlet.	
Students 4/5: Spokespeople	Prepare the team for presentation. Present pamphlet to the class.	

2. With your group, decide what information should go in your pamphlet, such as good health habits, types of doctors, nutrition, insurance information, and so on.

3. Write the text and decide on the art to use in your pamphlet.

4. Put your pamphlet together.

5. Present your pamphlet to the class.

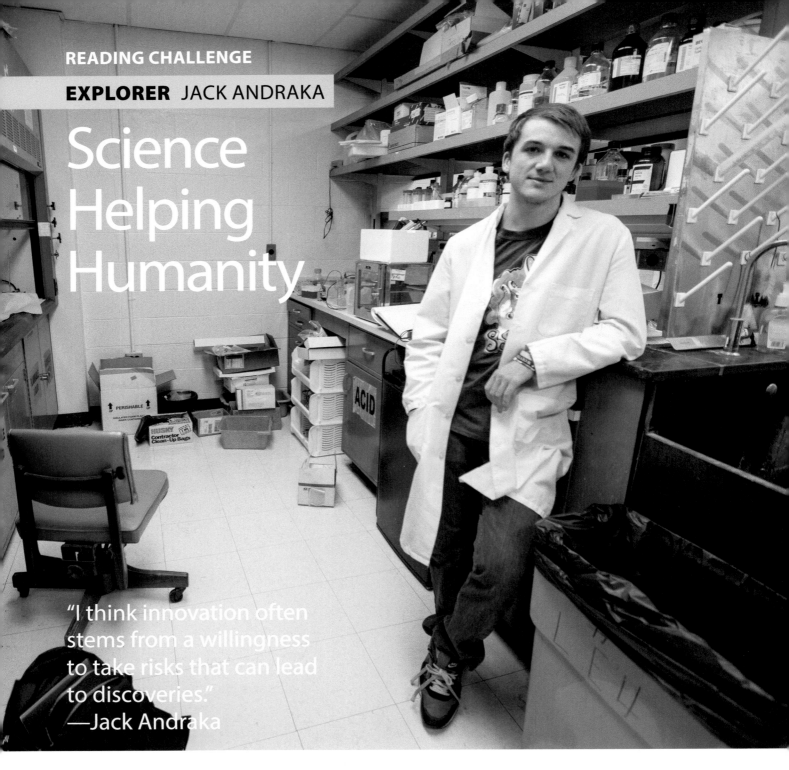

EXPLORER JACK ANDRAKA

Science Helping Humanity

"I think innovation often stems from a willingness to take risks that can lead to discoveries."
—Jack Andraka

A. PREDICT Look at the picture. Answer the questions.

1. How old do you think the person in the picture is? _____

2. What do you think he does? _____

3. Jack invented something that is 90% accurate, 168 times faster, 26,000 times cheaper, and 400 times more sensitive than what is currently available. What do you think he could have invented? _____

B. **Read about Jack Andraka.**

Jack Andraka is an inventor. He saw a problem and came up with a way to solve it, just like most inventors do. But Jack is not your typical inventor. When he was 15, not even out of high school yet, he did what most people never do. When a close family friend passed away due to pancreatic cancer, he decided to try to find a way to detect cancer earlier and to increase chances of survival. In Jack's words, "The fact that a hundred people die every day from the disease motivates me to not only work on my project, but also raise awareness of the need for more funding for research and for open access so more people can learn and innovate."

How did Jack find a way to do it? He was able to create a tool, a stick-like sensor, that detects an increase of protein. This increase in protein is related to the presence of certain cancers in their early stages. The earlier it is caught, the better the chance for a cure. This tool works for not only pancreatic cancer, which Jack's family friend passed away from, but also lung and ovarian cancer. The test takes about five minutes and only costs three cents to make.

Jack holds an international patent on his cancer detecting device and hopes that it will be available in the next ten years. He thinks the same detection method he invented could be applied to almost any disease. When asked what advice he would give to other people who want to make a difference, he said, "If I could have people do one thing, it would be to believe in the power of citizen scientists to innovate solutions to problems in their health and environment."

C. **Look at each vocabulary word and write its part of speech on the line: noun (N), verb (V), or adjective (A). Some can be more than one. Then, match each word to its correct meaning.**

1. innovate _____   a. money

2. funding _____   b. exclusive right given by the government to make and sell an invention

3. patent _____   c. a study of information about something

4. typical _____   d. heal, make someone healthy

5. sensor _____   e. a tool

6. research _____ , _____   f. create something new

7. detect _____   g. a substance used by an animal's body

8. cure _____ , _____   h. something that can detect a certain quality

9. device _____   i. uncover, find

10. protein _____   j. normal, average

D. **SUMMARIZE Using the information above, write a summary of what Jack Andraka has done in his life. Use transitions in your writing (*first, second, then, later,* etc.).**

Getting Hired

A female worker slides into the common room at the Google offices in Zurich, Switzerland.

UNIT OUTCOMES

- ☐ Identify skills and characteristics
- ☐ Conduct a job search
- ☐ Write a resume
- ☐ Write an e-mail
- ☐ Prepare for a job interview

Look at the photo and answer the questions.

1. What do you see in the picture?
2. What type of work are the people doing?
3. Why is there a slide?

LESSON ① What skills do you have?

GOAL ▮ Identify skills and characteristics

A. PREDICT Look at the pictures. What jobs are these people doing? Discuss them with a partner.

B. A *skill* is something you can do, such as use a computer or write a report. What skills are required for each job above? Discuss your ideas with a small group.

C. Below is a list of job titles. Work in groups to write the job responsibilities that go with each job. Then, add two more job titles to the list.

Job title	Job responsibilities
accountant	_____
administrative assistant	_____
assembler	_____
business owner	_____
cashier	_____
computer technician	repairs computers
delivery person	_____
dental assistant	_____
electrician	_____
firefighter	_____
garment worker	sews clothing
hairstylist	_____
homemaker	_____
landscape architect	_____
mail carrier	_____
receptionist	_____
reporter	_____
salesperson	_____
security guard	_____
_____	_____
_____	_____

D. Practice the conversation below using the information that you wrote in Exercise C.

Student A: What does a computer technician do?

Student B: A computer technician repairs computers.

E. DIFFERENTIATE In groups, discuss the difference between skills and characteristics. A *skill* is something you can do, such as change a tire or type a letter. A *characteristic* describes your personality and work habits, such as hardworking or well-organized. What are some other examples of characteristics?

F. Read some characteristics that employers look for in employees. Discuss the characteristics with your classmates and check (✓) the ones that describe you.

☐ a quick learner   ☐ creative   ☐ dependable

☐ detail-oriented   ☐ efficient   ☐ flexible

☐ good with numbers   ☐ great with people   ☐ hardworking

☐ well-organized   ☐ willing to accept responsibility   ☐ works well under pressure

G. Read the descriptions and choose a characteristic to describe each person.

1. Suzanne works long hours and never takes any breaks. _____

2. You can always rely on Linh. _____

3. Li is always calm, even when it's very stressful. _____

4. You never have to explain anything to Vlasta twice. _____

🎧 **H.** **SUPPOSE** Listen to four people describe their skills, characteristics, and interests. Take notes in the first column. Then, suggest a job for each person in the second column.

CD 1
TR 23

	Skills, characteristics, interests	Most suitable job
Lam		
Lilia		
Morteza		
Hilda		

I. Make a list of your skills and interests in your notebook. List at least three jobs that you might enjoy and be good at. Then, list the characteristics that make you good for each job.

L E S S O N ② Looking for a job

GOAL ■ Conduct a job search

A. What is the best way to look for a job? Make a list of different ways to look for a job.

Ways to Look for a Job

B. Make a list of things you need to think about before you begin your job search. Compare it with a partner.

1. hours available to work

2. _____

3. _____

4. _____

5. _____

6. _____

C. **CLASSIFY** What information is usually included in job ads? What information do you usually need to ask about? Put the information in the correct column.

benefits	job location	required skills
contact information	job title	salary/pay
how to apply	possibility of overtime	vacation
job hours	required qualifications	

Information found in the ad	Information I need to ask about
contact information	

D. Think about the job you have now. (Some of you may be students or homemakers. If you are, these are your jobs. If you are retired or unemployed, think about your last job.) Complete the column with information about your job.

	Information About Your Job
Job title	
Job location	
Job skills	
Qualifications	
Hours	
Salary	
Benefits	

E. **FIND OUT** Interview your classmates about their jobs. Write questions for each piece of information. Then, ask your classmates the questions and complete the columns.

Interview questions	Classmate 1	Classmate 2	Classmate 3
Title: What is your job title?			
Location:			
Skills:			
Qualifications:			
Hours:			
Benefits:			

F. Imagine that you want to work for a company. It is important to find out some information about the company or business ahead of time. Fill in the table.

What kind of information is useful to know?	Where can you find this information?
1. the number of employees who work for the company	1. on the company's website
2.	2.
3.	3.
4.	4.
5.	5.
6.	6.

G. VISUALIZE Think of the perfect job for you. Complete the table with what you want from that perfect job.

Job title	
Job location	
Size of company	
Hours	
Salary	
Benefits	
Other	

H. Share with your class and ask for ideas on where to look for a job like this.

LESSON ③ Resumes

GOAL ■ Write a resume

A. Read about Ranjit.

Ranjit Ghosh is from India. He moved to the United States seven years ago. In India, he attended the National Computer School and received a certificate in computer repair. His first job was troubleshooting computer repairs for a financial company. After he moved to the United States, he started assembling computers and was able to use the skills he had learned in his course in India. Although he loved his job, he needed another job to pay the bills. In addition to assembling computers, now he also repairs computers in the evenings for another company. Ranjit is busy, but he is doing what he loves.

B. Answer the questions about Ranjit.

1. Ranjit has had three jobs. List them with the most recent first.

   a. _____

   b. _____

   c. _____

2. Where did he go to school and what did he receive?

   _____

3. Why does Ranjit have two jobs in the United States?

   _____

C. RECALL Think about your job history. List your jobs starting with the most recent first.

1. _____ 2. _____

3. _____ 4. _____

5. _____ 6. _____

D. Read Ranjit's resume.

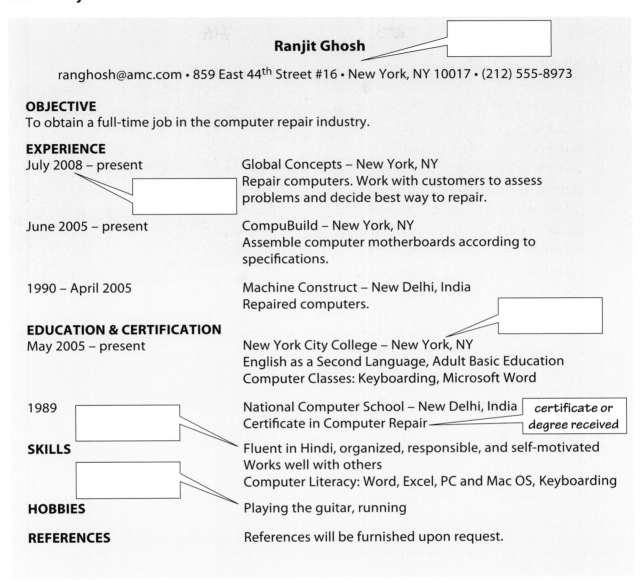

Ranjit Ghosh

ranghosh@amc.com • 859 East 44th Street #16 • New York, NY 10017 • (212) 555-8973

OBJECTIVE
To obtain a full-time job in the computer repair industry.

EXPERIENCE

July 2008 – present   Global Concepts – New York, NY
                             Repair computers. Work with customers to assess
                             problems and decide best way to repair.

June 2005 – present   CompuBuild – New York, NY
                             Assemble computer motherboards according to
                             specifications.

1990 – April 2005   Machine Construct – New Delhi, India
                             Repaired computers.

EDUCATION & CERTIFICATION

May 2005 – present   New York City College – New York, NY
                             English as a Second Language, Adult Basic Education
                             Computer Classes: Keyboarding, Microsoft Word

1989   National Computer School – New Delhi, India   certificate or
                             Certificate in Computer Repair   degree received

SKILLS   Fluent in Hindi, organized, responsible, and self-motivated
                             Works well with others
                             Computer Literacy: Word, Excel, PC and Mac OS, Keyboarding

HOBBIES   Playing the guitar, running

REFERENCES   References will be furnished upon request.

E. Can you identify the parts of a resume? Use the words below to label Ranjit's resume.

certificate or degree received	languages	name of school
computer skills	location of company	names of classes taken
dates of education	location of school	skills
dates of job	name and address	things you enjoy doing
job responsibilities	name of company	

F. ANALYZE Look at the words in the box in Exercise E. Why is it important to put each of the pieces of information on your resume? Discuss the reasons with a group and make notes about each item.

G. Think about your own resume. Fill in your information.

1. Schools you have attended: _____

_____

_____

2. Classes you have taken: _____

_____

_____

3. Certificates or degrees you have received: _____

_____

4. Awards you have received: _____

_____

5. Names and locations of companies you have worked for: _____

_____

_____

6. Job titles and responsibilities you have had: _____

_____

_____

7. Special characteristics you have: _____

_____

_____

8. Things you enjoy doing: _____

_____

_____

H. Using the information you wrote in Exercise G, write your resume on a piece of paper.

LESSON **4** **Cover letters**

GOAL ▪ Write an e-mail

A. Read the e-mail that Ranjit wrote when he sent his resume. What is the purpose of this e-mail?

Computer Technician Needed

Qualified, experienced computer technician to maintain equipment and operation. Dynamic, friendly work environment, and full benefits. Send cover letter and resume to:

Jane Hawkins
Trizon Electronics
497 West 67th Street, Fifth floor
New York, NY 10017

Send Now   Send Later   Save as Draft   Delete

June 14, 2016

To:
Cc:
Subject:

Dear Ms. Hawkins, — *Greeting*

Identify the position you wish to apply for.

I am writing in response to the ad for a computer technician advertised in the *New York Times* this past Sunday. I have the education and qualifications you are looking for and would be an asset to your team.

Outline your key strengths and abilities for this job.

As you can see from my attached resume, I have a certificate in computer repair and experience working on computers. I'm a hard worker and willing to learn new things. Trizon Electronics is a well-known, well-respected company, which I feel could teach me a lot. My schedule is flexible and I'd be willing to work whenever you need me.

Thank you for taking the time to consider my application. I will follow up next week with a phone call. I look forward to meeting you and discussing any opportunities there may be for me at your company. *Suggest next steps.*

Sincerely,

Ranjit Ghosh — *Closing*

B. Read the following job descriptions.

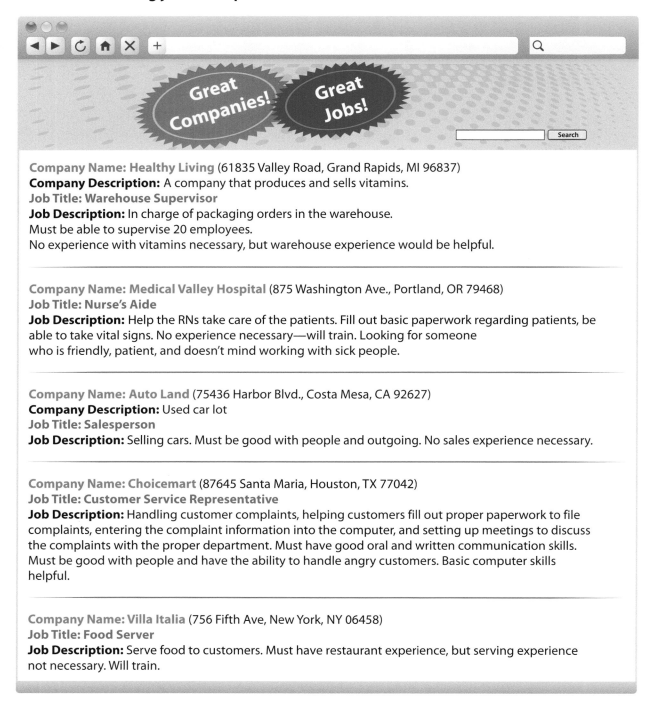

Company Name: Healthy Living (61835 Valley Road, Grand Rapids, MI 96837)
Company Description: A company that produces and sells vitamins.
Job Title: Warehouse Supervisor
Job Description: In charge of packaging orders in the warehouse.
Must be able to supervise 20 employees.
No experience with vitamins necessary, but warehouse experience would be helpful.

Company Name: Medical Valley Hospital (875 Washington Ave., Portland, OR 79468)
Job Title: Nurse's Aide
Job Description: Help the RNs take care of the patients. Fill out basic paperwork regarding patients, be able to take vital signs. No experience necessary—will train. Looking for someone who is friendly, patient, and doesn't mind working with sick people.

Company Name: Auto Land (75436 Harbor Blvd., Costa Mesa, CA 92627)
Company Description: Used car lot
Job Title: Salesperson
Job Description: Selling cars. Must be good with people and outgoing. No sales experience necessary.

Company Name: Choicemart (87645 Santa Maria, Houston, TX 77042)
Job Title: Customer Service Representative
Job Description: Handling customer complaints, helping customers fill out proper paperwork to file complaints, entering the complaint information into the computer, and setting up meetings to discuss the complaints with the proper department. Must have good oral and written communication skills. Must be good with people and have the ability to handle angry customers. Basic computer skills helpful.

Company Name: Villa Italia (756 Fifth Ave, New York, NY 06458)
Job Title: Food Server
Job Description: Serve food to customers. Must have restaurant experience, but serving experience not necessary. Will train.

C. GIVE SUPPORT Choose one job that you would like to apply for from the descriptions in Exercise B. Tell your partner why you would be good for this job.

D. IMAGINE Imagine that you are applying for the job that you chose in Exercise C. Write an e-mail to the company.

| Send Now | Send Later | Save as Draft | Delete | Add Attachment | Signature |

To:

Cc:

Subject:

_____

_____,

_____

_____

_____

_____

_____

_____

_____

_____

LESSON 5 Interviewing

GOAL ■ Prepare for a job interview

A. PLAN Now that you have written your resume and your cover letter, it's time to get ready for the interview! The best way to prepare for an interview is to practice.

Look at the sample interview questions below. How would you answer them? Discuss each question with a group. Then, write your answers on a piece of paper.

1. What can you tell me about yourself?

2. Why are you applying for this job?

3. Why do you think you would be good at this job?

4. What is your greatest strength?

5. What is your greatest weakness?

6. Do you prefer to work alone or with other people?

7. Why did you leave your last job?

8. What did you do at your last job?

9. What did you like most about your last job?

10. Describe a situation where you had a conflict with another employee. How did you solve it?

11. What special skills do you have that would benefit our company?

12. What characteristics do you have that would make you a good employee?

13. Do you have any questions?

B. With a partner, practice asking and answering the interview questions. Since you are just practicing, it is OK to look at the answers you wrote in Exercise A.

C. DETERMINE Read the list below and discuss with a partner what you think an employer is looking for.

Handshake ☐

Appearance ☐

Eye contact with interviewer ☐

Voice level (volume) ☐

Facial expressions ☐

Posture / body position ☐

Self-confidence / comfort level ☐

Willingness to volunteer information ☐

Appropriateness of responses to questions ☐

Effectiveness in describing strengths, skills, and abilities ☐

D. EVALUATE Looking at the list above, which two aspects are your strongest?

1. _____

2. _____

E. EVALUATE Which two aspects do you need to work on the most?

1. _____

2. _____

F. Now, it's time to practice. You will be interviewing for the job that you wrote your cover letter for. Work with a partner. Take turns being the interviewer and the interviewee.

Student A: Interviewer
Ask your partner at least ten of the questions on page 150. When the interview is over, fill out the mock interview evaluation form on page 152 in your partner's book.

Student B: Interviewee
Do your best to answer the questions without looking at your notes and try to do well on each of the aspects listed in Exercise C.

G. Fill out the mock evaluation form about your partner.

MOCK INTERVIEW EVALUATION FORM

Name of applicant: _____

Name of interviewer: _____

Date of interview: _____

Job applied for: _____

Rate the applicant on each of the following questions by writing *excellent, good,* or *fair.*

What kind of impression did this person make? _____
Did the person give answers that would make an employer want to hire him or her?

_____

Did the person have a friendly, enthusiastic, and positive attitude?

_____

Rate the applicant on the criteria below on a scale of 1 to 5.
(1 = poor, 5 = excellent)

CRITERIA	Rating				
	1	2	3	4	5
1. Handshake	____	____	____	____	____
2. Appearance	____	____	____	____	____
3. Eye contact with interviewer	____	____	____	____	____
4. Voice level (volume)	____	____	____	____	____
5. Facial expressions	____	____	____	____	____
6. Posture / body position	____	____	____	____	____
7. Self-confidence / comfort level	____	____	____	____	____
8. Willingness to volunteer information	____	____	____	____	____
9. Appropriateness of responses to questions	____	____	____	____	____
10. Effectiveness in describing strengths, skills, and abilities	____	____	____	____	____
11. Overall evaluation	____	____	____	____	____

What suggestions can you give this person for how to make a better impression?

_____

Additional comments: _____

_____

_____

▶ # Tell me about your job

Before You Watch

A. **Look at the picture. Complete each sentence.**

1. Hector has a pen, a notepad, and a

   tape _____.

2. Hector is _____ Naomi.

3. He wants to know about

   _____.

While You Watch

B. ▶ **Watch the video. Complete the dialog.**

Mr. Sanchez: I'm a (1) _loan officer_ .

Hector: What does that mean?

Mr. Sanchez: When customers want to get a loan—that is, when they want to (2) _____ money—they come to see me. I look at their credit and decide if they qualify.

Hector: Sometimes you must have to give people (3) _____ .

Mr. Sanchez: Yes, you're right about that. Sometimes I *do* have to give bad news, and that's hard. But sometimes I have good news for an (4) _____ . Yesterday, for example, I told a young couple that they qualified for a home loan. They were so excited. This was a big event in their life. And I got to be a part of it.

Hector: It must be very (5) _____ to help people like that.

Check Your Understanding

C. **Read the statements. Write T for *True* or F for *False*.**

1. Hector is writing an article for the Glendale newspaper.   _F_

2. Naomi likes talking to people in her job.   _____

3. Naomi says being on her feet all day is tiring.   _____

4. Mr. Sanchez sometimes has to give people bad news in his job.   _____

5. Mr. Patel first worked at his father's store.   _____

Review

Learner Log

I can identify skills and characteristics of a good employee.
☐ Yes ☐ Maybe ☐ No

I can conduct a job search.
☐ Yes ☐ Maybe ☐ No

A. Write job responsibilities for the job titles.

Job title	Job responsibilities
administrative assistant	_____
cashier	_____
delivery person	_____
dental assistant	_____
electrician	_____
homemaker	_____
receptionist	_____
salesperson	_____

B. List six characteristics you think an employer is looking for in an employee.

1. _____   2. _____

3. _____   4. _____

5. _____   6. _____

C. Imagine you are looking for a job. Complete the table about your ideal job.

Information about Your Ideal Job	
Job title	
Job location	
Job skills	
Qualifications	
Hours	
Salary	
Benefits	

D. **List ten pieces of information that go on a resume.**

1. _____   2. _____

3. _____   4. _____

5. _____   6. _____

7. _____   8. _____

9. _____   10. _____

E. **How would you answer these interview questions? Write your answers below.**

1. What is your greatest strength? _____

_____

2. What is your greatest weakness? _____

_____

3. What special skills do you have that would benefit our company?

_____

_____

4. What characteristics do you have that would make you a good employee?

_____

_____

5. What did you like most about your last job?

_____

_____

F. **If you want to get a job, what are all the things you need to do from beginning to end? List them below.**

1. _Write a resume._ _____

2. _____

3. _____

4. _____

5. _____

6. _____

G. **In this unit, you learned many things about getting a job. With a group, discuss the following. Complete the sentences to explain why each one is important. Share your answers with the class.**

1. Knowing what my skills are is important because _____

_____.

2. Finding information about the job I want is important because _____

_____.

3. Finding information about the company I am applying to is important because

_____

_____.

4. Writing a resume is important because _____

_____.

5. Writing a cover letter is important because _____

_____.

6. Practicing interviewing is important because _____

_____.

H. **Take out your dictionary and add a section about yourself. Make two lists—one for your skills and one for your characteristics. Write down anything you can do and anything that describes you. If you need to add definitions for any of the words, put them in the same section. Use these lists as a reference when applying for a job or school.**

Skills	Characteristics
_____	_____
_____	_____
_____	_____
_____	_____
_____	_____
_____	_____

TEAM PROJECT ✓ # Create a job application portfolio

Part 1: By yourself, you will create a job application portfolio that will contain all the information you need to apply for a job and go to a practice interview.

1. List all of the information you want to include in your portfolio.

2. Create the different parts of your portfolio.
   - All portfolios must include the following: a resume, a cover letter, and sample interview questions and answers.
   - Other items that might be included in the portfolio: certificates, awards, transcripts, performance reviews, letters of recommendation.

Create a job advertisement and conduct interviews

Part 2: With a team, you will write a brief job advertisement and interview other students for that job.

1. **COLLABORATE** Form a team with four students. Choose positions for each member of your team.

Position	Job description	Student name
Student 1: Company Owner	Check that everyone speaks English and participates.	
Student 2: Department Supervisor	Write job advertisement and interview questions.	
Student 3: Company President	Ask interview questions.	
Students 4: Human Resources Director	Create evaluation form.	

2. Decide what company you work for and for what position you are hiring. Write a job advertisement for the position.

3. Prepare a list of interview questions that you will ask the applicants.

4. Decide what you are looking for in an employee and create an evaluation form.

5. Once your classmates have seen all of the job advertisements and decided on a job to apply for, interview and evaluate the applicants.

6. Choose the best person for the job.

EXPLORER THOMAS TAHA RASSAM CULHANE

Solar Power with Locally Produced Innovative Ideas

"We're not being idealistic; we're out to provide solutions."
—Thomas Taha Rassam Culhane

A. Answer the following questions with a small group.

1. How long does it take you to fill up your bathtub with hot water?

2. How long does it take your shower to get hot?

B. PREDICT What do you think Thomas Culhane is doing in the picture?

C. Read about Thomas Culhane.

In some communities, a mother spends up to seven hours bathing her children. She doesn't have a hot water heater (or running water for that matter), so she has to fill buckets of water from the neighborhood pipe, carry the buckets up the stairs to her apartment, and then heat it on the stove. How can she get anything else done if she has to spend her entire day making hot water to help keep her family clean?

Thomas Taha Rassam "T.H." Culhane and his wife moved to a slum apartment in Cairo so they could experience life like its residents. He decided there had to be a better way and figured out how to produce and install rooftop solar water heaters. "They generate 200 liters of hot water and 200 liters of cold water for each household every day," Culhane explains. Almost as great as the water being generated is that the community is working together to build the heaters from scratch, all from recycled materials. "We realize the value of collective intelligence. These neighborhoods are filled with welders, plumbers, carpenters, and glassworkers. We bring capital and plans; they bring talent and creativity."

The people of Cairo are called Zabaleen, which is translated as "garbage people," because they collect and recycle the city's waste by hand. They had thought about solar heaters to solve their problem, but for them to buy one solar heater would have cost them a whole year's salary. When Thomas came in with his basic design plans, the local craftsmen improved upon the plans and figured out how to produce it with locally recycled materials. Culhane has a belief that poor communities are rich with possibilities and innovative ideas. The Zabaleen people of Cairo proved this to be true.

D. Answer the questions.

1. What is the problem for the people of Cairo who live in the slums?

_____

2. What solution did Thomas Culhane come up with?

_____

3. How did the Zabaleen people help Thomas?

_____

E. SOLVE Work with a small group to come up with a problem in your house that is too expensive for you to fix. How could you solve it in an inexpensive way? As a group, write a short paragraph explaining the problem and solution.

On the Job

The saw squad
pauses for their
annual photo
on a massive
Douglas fir in
Butte, Montana.

UNIT OUTCOMES

☐ Identify different types
of workplace behavior

☐ Identify workplace actions

☐ Communicate problems
to a supervisor

☐ Make ethical decisions

☐ Ask for a raise

**Look at the photo and
answer the questions.**

1. What is a saw squad?

2. What skills do these workers
need?

3. What type of workplace
behavior is necessary for
this job?

GOAL ■ Identify different types of workplace behavior

A. DECIDE Imagine that you are at work. Think carefully about each action below and decide if it is appropriate (A) or inappropriate (I) workplace behavior. Write *A* or *I* next to each statement.

_A_ Ask a coworker for help.

_A_ Ask for a raise.

_A_ Ask your <u>supervisor</u> a question.

_A_ Call in sick (when you are really sick).

_I_ Send personal e-mails.

_I_ Sit on your desk.

_A_ Come back from break early.

_I_ Smoke while you're working.

_I_ Talk to a friend on the phone.

_I_ Do Internet research for your child's school project.

_I_ Take products home for your friends and family.

_A_ Talk to your boss about a problem with a coworker.

_I_ Arrive a few minutes late.

_A_ Tell your boss you don't understand something he or she said.

B. Discuss your answers with a group and think of three more examples of both appropriate and inappropriate workplace behavior. Share your ideas with the class.

_____

_____

_____

C. COMPARE Read the two questions. Which is a tag question?

"Is she late for work?"

I have no idea, but I want to know.

"She's late for work again, isn't she?"

I'm not 100% sure, but I think this is true.

D. Read the questions and answers below about the tag question.

Tag question: She's late for work again, isn't she?

Q: Why is this called a tag question?

A: Because it's a question tagged onto the end of a sentence.

Q: When do we use tag questions?

A: When we are almost sure something is true, but we want to check and be 100% sure.

Q: When I'm asking a tag question, how do I know if the tag should be positive or negative?

A: If the sentence is positive, the tag is negative. If the sentence is negative, the tag is positive.

Q: What verb tense do I use in the tag?

A: Use the same verb tense in the tag that is used in the beginning of the statement.

E. Study the chart with your teacher.

Tag Questions			
Positive statement	**Tag**	**Negative statement**	**Tag**
She works,	doesn't she?	She doesn't work,	does she?
She is working,	isn't she?	She isn't working,	is she?
She worked,	didn't she?	She didn't work,	did she?
She will work,	won't she?	She won't work,	will she?
She is going to work,	isn't she?	She isn't going to work,	is she?
She has worked,	hasn't she?	She hasn't worked,	has she?
She had worked,	hadn't she?	She hadn't worked,	had she?

F. Complete the questions with the correct tag.

1. He isn't e-mailing a friend, _is he_ ?

2. Lisa and Jack have never missed a day of work, _have they_ ?

3. Maria works late every night, _doesn't she_ ?

4. Our coworkers will be fired next week, _won't they_ ?

5. My assistant is going to eat lunch during the meeting, _isn't ~~she~~ he_ ?

6. She didn't finish her work, _did she_ ?

7. The supervisor said to wait until tomorrow to ask for a raise, _didn't she_ ?

8. He wore shorts to his interview, _didn't he_ ?

9. Roberto had stolen things before, _hadn't he_ ?

10. We'll have a business meeting next week, _won't we_ ?

G. Listen to the tag questions. Check (✓) the tag that you hear.

1. ☐ did he?   ☑ didn't he?   ☐ does he?   ☐ doesn't he?

2. ☐ won't she?   ☐ will she?   ☑ won't we?   ☐ don't we?

3. ☑ did they?   ☐ did he?   ☐ didn't they?   ☐ didn't he?

4. ☐ hasn't she?   ☐ did she?   ☐ didn't she?   ☑ has she?

5. ☐ are you?   ☑ aren't you?   ☐ weren't you?   ☐ were you?

H. Write three tag questions about inappropriate workplace behavior.

1. She told her boss he looked bad, didn't she?
2. He used his Phone, didn't he?
3. She eating in the Kitchen, doesn't she?
4. He coming late everying day, does he?

I. Write three tag questions about appropriate workplace behavior.

1. She wore a suit to the interview, didn't she?
2. She cleaning every day so good, does she?
3. He coming early at Work, does he?
4. They maded a good Job the last week, didn't they?

LESSON ② The note was written by Jim

Past

GOAL ▪ Identify workplace actions

🎧 **A.** **Look at the picture. Where are these people? What are they talking about? What can you see on the desk? Then, read and listen to the conversation.**

CD 1
TR 25

Raquel: Did you see the note I put on your screen?

Bruno: Was that note from you? I thought it was put there by Jim.

Raquel: Actually, the note was written by Jim, but I taped it to your screen. I wanted to make sure you got it before you left for lunch.

Bruno: I did get it. The orders were sent to me yesterday, and I'll have them ready for your signature before I leave today.

Raquel: Great! I'll sign them in the morning, and then you can send them to the finance department. Make sure they are sent by Package Express.

Bruno: I'll take care of it right away.

B. **Answer the questions about the conversation.**

1. Who are the two people in the conversation? Who is the supervisor?

2. What was the misunderstanding?

3. What was sent to Bruno?

C. **CHANGE Practice the conversation again, but this time replace some of the words and phrases with the new words below.**

screen	→	computer
note	→	memo
lunch	→	the day
the finance department	→	human resources
right away	→	as soon as possible

D. Study the chart. Compare the sentences in the passive voice with those in the active voice. What are the differences?

Passive voice	Active voice
The note **was put** there by Raquel.	Raquel **put** the note there.
The note **was written** by Jim.	Jim **wrote** the note.
The orders **were sent** yesterday. (We don't know who sent them.)	They **sent** the orders yesterday.

E. **DECIDE** Read each sentence and write *A* for active or *P* for passive.

1. The copy machine was repaired last week. ___P___

2. My manager wrote the report. ___A___

No hay Persona

3. The dishwashers were laid off by their supervisor. ___P___

Si hay Persona

4. Was the package received? ___P___

5. Eli designed the new brochure. ___A___
   S   V

6. The new office building was built last year. ___P___

7. Our new employees were given an orientation. ___P___

8. Kelli was given a raise last week. ___P___

9. James and Brian started their own business. ___A___

10. José quit. ___A___

F. Rewrite each sentence in the active voice. (*Hint*: Use the simple past tense.)

1. Three dishwashers were laid off by the supervisor.

   The supervisor laid off three dishwashers.

2. Our new employees were given an orientation by the manager.

   The manager gave an orientation to the New employee

3. Kelli was given a raise last week by the owner of the company.

   The owner of the Company gave Kelli a raise last week

4. The package was received by the receptionist.

   The receptionist received the package

G. Study the chart below.

Passive Voice				
Example sentence	Passive subject	*Be*	Past participle	(*By* + person or thing)
The note was written by Jim.	It	was	written	
The orders were sent yesterday. (We don't know who sent them.)	They	were	sent	by Jim

- Use the passive voice to emphasize the object of the action, or when the doer of the action is unknown or unimportant.
- To change an active sentence into a passive sentence, switch the subject and the object, and change the verb to the correct tense of *be* + the past participle. The word *by* is used before the doer of the action.

H. Change the sentences from active voice to passive voice.

1. Our delivery person brought twelve bottles of water this morning.

   Twelve bottles of water were brought by our delivery person this morning.

2. The receptionist bought all the supplies.

   All the Supplies were bought by the Receptions

3. The repairperson fixed the copy machine.

   The Copy machine was fixed by the Repairperson

4. Someone stole his money and driver's license.

   His money and drive's licen6e were Stolen

5. A nurse took my blood pressure.

   My blood Pressure was taken by nurse

I. **ANALYZE** Think of three things you did at work last week. Write three passive voice sentences.

1. The Kitchen was cleand by Will
2. The package was ~~sed~~ sent by the company
3. All the veggies was cut

GOAL ▨ Communicate problems to a supervisor

🎧 **A. Read and listen to the conversation.**
CD 1
TR 26

Construction Worker:	Excuse me, do you have a second?
Supervisor:	Sure. What is it?
Construction Worker:	Well, there's a small problem. The shipment of lumber didn't arrive, so we have to stop construction until it gets here. What would you like us to do?

Supervisor:	There's nothing else you can do while you are waiting for it?
Construction Worker:	No. We need that lumber to start working on the door frames.
Supervisor:	OK. Well, why don't you guys take lunch early, and I'll call and see where the lumber is.
Construction Worker:	Let me make sure I understand you correctly. You want all of us to go on lunch break right now while you call and find out where the lumber is?
Supervisor:	That's right.
Construction Worker:	When should we come back?
Supervisor:	In about an hour.
Construction Worker:	Thank you. See you in an hour.

B. Answer the questions about the conversation.

1. What is the problem?

2. What does the employee say to get the supervisor's attention?

3. Does the supervisor understand the problem?

4. What does he suggest they do to solve the problem?

How to get someone's attention politely	How to check that you have understood
Excuse me, sir/ma'am/(name). Do you have a minute? Pardon me, sir/ma'am/(name). Can I talk to you for a second?	Let me make sure I understand you. What you are saying is . . . So what we/I should do is . . .

C. INTERPRET Read the flowchart. Do you agree with each step?

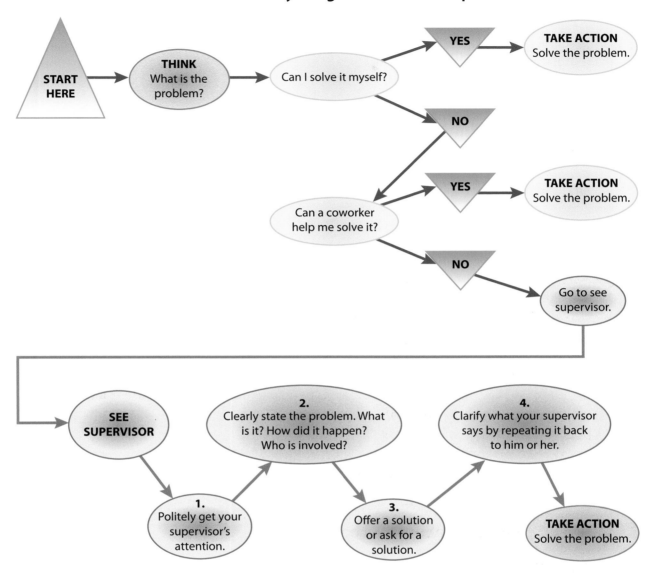

D. Discuss these questions with a partner.

1. If you can solve the problem by yourself, what should you do?

2. If a coworker can help you solve the problem, what should you do?

3. When you go to see your supervisor, what is the first thing you should do? What is the last thing you should do?

E. Look at the conversation on page 168. Did the construction worker follow the steps in the flowchart?

> **HOW TO OFFER A SOLUTION**
>
> Why don't we/I . . .
>
> What if we/I . . .
>
> Would it work if we/I . . .

F. DETERMINE With a group, read each situation below. Following the steps in the flowchart on page 169, discuss what you would do if you were in these situations.

1. Renee is a cashier in a fast-food restaurant. A customer just came up to the counter and told her that she gave him the wrong change. He doesn't have his receipt, and she doesn't remember helping him. What should she do?

2. Mikhail came back from lunch and found a message marked *urgent* on his desk, but it wasn't addressed to him. He doesn't recognize the name of the addressee so he doesn't know what to do with it. What should he do?

3. James and Sara assemble telephones. For this particular group of phones, they have an uneven amount of parts and aren't able to finish 20 of the phones. What should they do?

G. Separate your class into two groups. Read your group's directions.

Group A: Supervisors
As a group, discuss how you would solve each of the employees' problems below. Be prepared to communicate this to the employee when he or she asks you.

Group B: Employees
As a group, discuss what you would say to your supervisor about each of the problems below. Remember the four steps from the flowchart.

Problems

1. You just received your paycheck, and you notice that you didn't get paid for the overtime hours you worked.

2. There is an emergency phone call for you, but, if you leave your place, you will throw off the assembly line.

3. You are out installing cable TV at a customer's home, and the customer is unhappy with your service.

H. APPLY When you are ready, each supervisor from Group A should find an employee from Group B to talk to about the first problem. Make sure each employee talks to a different supervisor about each problem.

I. Switch roles. The supervisors will become employees, and the employees will become supervisors.

LESSON ④ What should you do?

GOAL ▪ Make ethical decisions

A. DECIDE Each situation below describes an ethical question that you might face. What would you do? Check (✓) your answers and discuss them with a partner.

DEFINITION

ethics: *n.* moral rules or principles of behavior for deciding what is right and wrong; *adj.* – **ethical**

1. You pay the cashier at the supermarket with a 10-dollar bill. He gives you change as if you had given him a 20-dollar bill. What would you do?

   ___✓___ Tell her.   _____ Keep the extra money.

2. It's the night before the final exam at your school and you haven't had much time to study. A classmate has stolen the answers to the exam and offers to share them with you. What would you do?

   ___✓___ Say no.   _____ Borrow the answers from him.

3. You go shopping and buy some books. When you get home, you realize that the clerk put an extra book in your bag that you didn't pay for. What would you do?

   ___✓___ Go back to the store and give the book back.   _____ Keep it.

B. In situations like the ones in Exercise A, you know what you should do, but do you always do it? Sometimes the decision is not easy, but there are steps you can take to help you make a good decision.

> **Steps for Making an Ethical Decision**
> 1. Identify the ethical issue or problem.
> 2. List the facts that are most relevant to your decision.
> 3. Identify the people who might be affected by your decision and how.
> 4. Explain what each person would want you to do about the issue.
> 5. List three different decisions you could make and what the outcome of each decision would be.
> 6. Decide what you will do.

C. Using the steps above, discuss one of the situations in Exercise A with a group and decide what would be the best thing to do.

D. JUDGE Read the situations below. Which one is the worst?

1. Ricardo, the night security guard, has access to all of the buildings at night. It is a slow night and he wants to check his personal e-mail using one of the available computers. The company has a strict policy about e-mail being used for business purposes only, but Ricardo is the only person in the building.

2. Emilia is a janitor who is in charge of cleaning the restrooms and refilling the supplies. She is the only one with a key to the supply closet. Her husband is very sick and she is having trouble making enough money to support her family. Often they can't afford food and they can't afford to buy toilet paper and soap.

3. Kimberly, who works as a receptionist in the front office, has access to the copy machine to make copies for other employees. Her daughter, Alyse, needs some copies for a school project. She brought her own paper and needs 200 copies for her class. She needs to have the copies or she will fail the project. The copier does not require a security code and they don't keep track of who makes how many copies.

4. Brandon works in Quality Control, helping refurbish used computers. Once a year, his supervisor gives away computers to a local elementary school. He doesn't keep any record of this, and Brandon really needs a computer for his son who is just starting high school. His supervisor asks him to deliver twelve computers to a local school.

E. APPLY Work with a partner and choose one of the situations from Exercise D. Follow the steps for making an ethical decision in Exercise B and answer the questions below.

1. What is the ethical problem?

   Bad Used The elements Company's

2. What are the relevant facts?

   Ricardo neglect his Job

3. Which people are involved and how would each person be affected?

   Ricardo and the Company

4. What would each person want you to do?

   Ricardo Should ~~use your~~ have the things personals in the time free or in his house

5. What are three different possible decisions?

   1. He can go and look his e-mail
   2. Wait finish the time Job
   3. He can look in other moment

6. What is your final decision?

   Abstain from seeing your e-mail.

F. REFLECT On a separate piece of paper, write a description of an actual situation where you had to make an ethical choice. What did you do? How did you feel afterward?

LESSON **5** A raise

A. **Discuss these questions with your group.**

1. Have you ever received a raise at your job? If yes, what was it for?

2. Have you ever asked for a raise? If yes, did you get it? If no, did your manager or supervisor explain to you why you didn't get it?

B. **SUPPOSE** Many people hesitate to ask for a raise. Can you think of some reasons why? List them.

_____

_____

_____

C. **Raj met with his boss yesterday to ask for a raise. Read about his experience.**

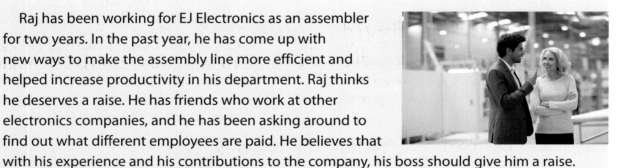

Raj has been working for EJ Electronics as an assembler for two years. In the past year, he has come up with new ways to make the assembly line more efficient and helped increase productivity in his department. Raj thinks he deserves a raise. He has friends who work at other electronics companies, and he has been asking around to find out what different employees are paid. He believes that with his experience and his contributions to the company, his boss should give him a raise.

First, Raj went to see Heidi in Human Resources and asked her what procedures he needed to follow to ask for a raise. She suggested that he make an appointment with his boss. So, last week, he asked his boss if the two of them could sit down and have a meeting. When his boss agreed, he began to gather his paperwork: job evaluations, memos from his supervisor about the new assembly-line configurations, his "Employee of the Month" award, and records of his attendance at work. He sat down and thought about all the questions his boss might ask him, and he wrote out detailed answers. Then, he asked his cousin to help him practice by asking him those questions.

D. **Answer the questions.**

1. Do you think Raj deserves a raise? Why or why not?

2. Who did he talk to first after he decided to ask for a raise? What did she tell him?

3. What did he do to prepare for the meeting with his boss?

E. Read the following article about getting a raise. Underline the advice that could be useful for you.

How to Ask for a Raise

Men are still earning more than women—lots more. According to the most recent data from the US Bureau of Labor Statistics, the gap between men and women is 18%. This means that a woman earns 82 cents for every dollar a man earns. In other words, a woman works four weeks to earn as much as her male counterpart earns in three weeks.

How can women close the gap? Knock on the boss's door and ask for a raise! Getting a raise is not as difficult as it might seem. Here are ten tips to assist women in negotiating their annual raise.

1. Be a star performer. Make yourself indispensable to the company. Document your successes by saving e-mails and letters, and then compile them into a portfolio. Make sure to take this portfolio with you when you go to your boss.

2. Do some research. Know what other men and women in your field are paid.

3. Focus on your contributions to the company. While the raise is certainly important to you, do not focus on how it will help your credit card debt.

4. Be informed. Know the company's policy on raises by asking your human resources director.

5. Timing is everything. Don't ask when the office is hectic; wait until the pace has slowed down and the moment is right.

6. Do your homework. Rehearse and prepare responses to counter any objections your boss might have. Know ahead of time what the difficult questions might be and have your answers ready.

7. Rehearse. If you can, role-play the scenario with a friend or colleague. This will help you become more comfortable when you are actually face-to-face with your boss.

8. Be professional. Ask for a formal meeting with your boss.

9. Cover your bases. Make four points about your contributions prior to asking for the raise. Illustrate your ability
- to find solutions,
- to go above and beyond your job responsibilities,
- to help others, and, most important,
- to increase the company's profitability.

10. Don't take *no* for an answer. Negotiate more vacation time, stock options, 401K contribution, or flextime. Set goals and ask for another review in three months.

F. **ANALYZE** Discuss these questions with a group.

1. This article focuses on how women should ask for a raise. Do you think these same ideas apply to men? Why or why not?

2. Which aspect of asking for a raise do you think is the most difficult? Take a poll among your group members.

G. **Read the memo that Rogelio wrote to his supervisor asking for a raise.**

Dear Mr. Michalski,

    I'm writing this letter to ask you to consider giving me a raise. I have been working at Mitchel George Manufacturing for five years, and I really like my job here. I started out as a warehouse packer, and now I work in the shipping department.

    I feel like I deserve a raise because, in the past year, I have been given more responsibilities on my shift. I have trained ten new employees and become a team leader. I have increased efficiency in my department by implementing a new flow system that helps us pack and ship the boxes in less time. Therefore, I hope that you will consider giving me a raise.

    I would like to sit down and discuss this possibility with you as soon as it is convenient for you. Thank you for your time.

Sincerely,

Rogelio Rodriguez

H. **Read the letter again and check (✓) the items Rogelio included in his letter.**

✓ _thank you_ to his supervisor for reading the letter

✓ reason for the letter

✓ how long he has been working for the company

_____ what his job is

_____ how his job has changed since he has been there

✓ things he has done to help the company

I. **You can ask for a raise in person or by writing a letter or e-mail. What are the advantages and disadvantages of each method?**

J. **EVALUATE** **Let's get ready to ask for a raise! First, answer these questions. (If you are a homemaker or a student, imagine that you get paid for what you do and are asking for more money.)**

1. Do you deserve a raise? Why or why not?

2. How long have you been working at your job?

3. When was the last time you got a raise?

4. Have you been working harder or working more hours?

5. Have you been given more responsibilities?

6. Have you gotten good reviews from your supervisors?

K. **Work with a partner to practice asking for a raise, or write a letter asking for a raise.**

I think you gave the wrong change

Before You Watch

A. Look at the picture. Complete each sentence.

1. The customer _is a men_.

2. He is _looking_ the store.

3. It's important to _buy something_ before you leave a store.

While You Watch

B. ▶ Watch the video. Complete the dialog.

Hector:	And the tie (1) _was_ $22?
Customer:	That's (2) _Right_.
Hector:	And you gave me $30, (3) _gaven't you?_ didn't you?
Customer:	No, I (4) _didn't_. I gave you $40.
Hector:	You mean two $20 (5) _bills_ ?
Customer:	(6) _Correct_.

Check Your Understanding

C. Read the statements. Write T for _True_ or F for _False_.

1. The customer wants to buy a tie for $22.   _T_

2. The customer counts the change Hector gives him.   _T_

3. Hector thinks the customer gave him $30.   _T_

4. Mateo gives the customer $10.   _F_

5. Mr. Patel is angry with Hector.   _F_

Review

Learner Log

I can identify different types of workplace behavior.
☐ Yes ☐ Maybe ☐ No

I can identify workplace actions.
☐ Yes ☐ Maybe ☐ No

A. Add tags to the statements to make tag questions.

1. She is going to ask for a promotion, __isn't she__ ?
2. We will volunteer to help them finish, __Won't we__ ?
3. Ken gets to work early every day, __doesn't he__ ?
4. Her sister can't pass her drug test, __Can she__ ?
5. They won't get that project done on time, __Will they__ ?

B. List two examples of appropriate and inappropriate employee behavior.

Appropriate Employee Behavior:
1. Come to work early
2. Talk with Supervisor for help

Inappropriate Employee Behavior:
1. Use your the Phone On the Job
2. Sleep in the Job

C. Use the words below to write sentences in the passive voice.

1. new office building / build / Lynn Street

   A new office building was built on Lynn Street.

2. childcare workers / give / a raise Childcare Workers were given a Raise

   a raise was given to childcare workers

3. machines / repair / mechanics

   The machines were repaired by Mechanics

4. computer / buy / the finance department

   The Computer was bought by the finance department

5. reports / write / two weeks ago

   The Reports were Written in two week ago

6. package / sent / express mail

   The Package was Sent by express mail

D. What are two ways to politely get someone's attention? Write them below.

1. _____
2. _____

Learner Log

I can communicate problems to supervisors.   I can make ethical decisions.
■ Yes   ■ Maybe   ■ No   ■ Yes   ■ Maybe   ■ No

E.   **Recall how to communicate a problem to a supervisor. Circle the best answer.**

1. What is the first step in communicating a problem to a supervisor?

   a. Take action.

   b. Think about what the problem is.

   c. Offer a solution.

2. What should you do if you can solve the problem yourself?

   a. Take action and solve the problem yourself.

   b. Ask a coworker for help.

   c. Offer a solution.

3. What should you do if you and your coworker can't solve the problem yourselves?

   a. Take action.

   b. Think about what the problem is.

   c. Go see your supervisor.

4. What is the first thing you should do when you talk to your supervisor?

   a. Ask for a solution.

   b. Think about what the problem is.

   c. Politely get his or her attention.

5. After your supervisor offers a solution, what should you do?

   a. Ask for a solution.

   b. Clarify what your supervisor has said by repeating it back to him or her.

   c. Take action and solve the problem.

F.   **What are the six steps to making an ethical decision? List them below.**

1. _____

2. _____

3. _____

4. _____

5. _____

6. _____

G.　Read the situation. Based on the steps you wrote in Exercise F, what would you do?

> You work in a restaurant and notice that your coworker is taking food off of the customers' plates before they are served—a french fry here, a carrot there. You know that your coworker is supporting a very large family and doesn't have enough money to feed everyone. What would you do?

_____

_____

_____

H.　You read ten suggestions on how to ask for a raise. List them in your own words.

1. _____
2. _____
3. _____
4. _____
5. _____
6. _____
7. _____
8. _____
9. _____
10. _____

I.　Can you think of synonyms for these words? Use a dictionary if you need help. Synonyms are words that have the same or similar meanings.

problem—*difficulty, hard time*

solution—*answer, explanation*

fact　_____

decision　_____

rehearse　_____

illustrate　_____

contributions　_____

With a team, you will solve a company problem in an action committee and create a handout for the class.

1. **COLLABORATE** Form a human resources action committee with four or five students. Choose positions for each member of your team.

Position	Job description	Student name
Student 1: **Human Resources Director**	Check that everyone speaks English and participates.	
Student 2: **Secretary**	Take notes and write information for handout.	
Student 3: **Designer**	Prepare final handout.	
Students 4/5: **Spokespeople**	Report final decision to the class.	

2. With your group, carefully read the problem below.

3. Use the steps for making an ethical decision from page 172 as you consider each possible solution.

4. Make a final decision.

5. Create a handout explaining the process you went through to come up with your decision.

6. Report your final decision to the class.

Company: RB Aerospace—Refurbishes and designs airplane interiors

Problem: A group of employees discovers that the quality of some of the parts they are using is not up to standard. They are worried that this may cause safety problems when the aircraft is in use. They have mentioned it to the quality control supervisor, but the factory is on a tight schedule and if they don't deliver this contract on time, they may lose future contracts.

EXPLORER CATHERINE JAFFEE

Producing Food and Preserving the Environment

"The thing I love most about bees is that, above all else, they are a creature of stories; small stories, about food, pollen and nectar, big stories, about threats to the hive, mating, and moving."
—Catherine Jaffee

A. Catherine Jaffee thinks that sharing stories builds communities and gives our lives purpose. Why does this happen?

B. DISCOVER Work with a small group to find out the meaning of the words/phrases below.

food anthropologist: _____

beekeeper: _____

heritage: _____

ancient traditions: _____

isolated: _____

local food systems: _____

C. Read about Catherine Jaffee's work.

Catherine loves bees. So much so that she moved to Turkey and helped build a honey-tasting walking heritage route. While studying in Turkey, she discovered fields full of beekeepers—people with ancient beekeeping traditions making honey that changed in taste every few kilometers. She came up with the idea to help women in these rural villages make a living by making honey.

Her day starts at 5 a.m. and ends at 9 p.m. She eats breakfast with the shepherds, milks cows, and walks the high mountain trails, moving from beekeeper to beekeeper. Midday, she takes a nap in a tent on top of sheep fluff and eats a lunch of cheese, bread, olives, tomatoes, apricots, and nuts. Then, she helps women cook, clean, and take care of the children before they harvest and clean hives. In the evening, she boils water for a shower, cleans her clothes, and after dinner falls asleep in a room of five or six little girls. And then, she wakes up and does it all over again.

Catherine's favorite experiences have been watching her beekeeper friends grow and change with their bees. Because she visits the same families over and over, she becomes very close to them and feels like a special member of their families. The hardest part of her job is the lifestyle in eastern Turkey. The roads are bad, the climate is harsh, and she often feels very isolated.

As a food anthropologist, Catherine is very passionate and asks that we as consumers do two things. "Know where your food is coming from and support your local food producers. The best thing we can be is smart food consumers. Take the time and effort to inform yourself on your local food systems, to become involved in what you eat, grow, and plant, and make an effort to connect with other people around good food and the natural growing world around us."

D. Answer the questions in a small group.

1. How is Catherine's day different than yours?

2. The third paragraph talks about the good and bad of Catherine's job. Do you think the good outweighs the bad? In what way?

3. How do you think Catherine's work with beekeepers connects to her quote at the end of the reading?

E. JUSTIFY Reread the paragraph about Catherine's day. If you could get paid to do this for your career, would you? Why or why not? On a separate piece of paper, write a paragraph explaining your reasons.

Civic
Responsibility

Tourists walk at dusk around the
Martin Luther King, Jr. Memorial
in Washington, DC.

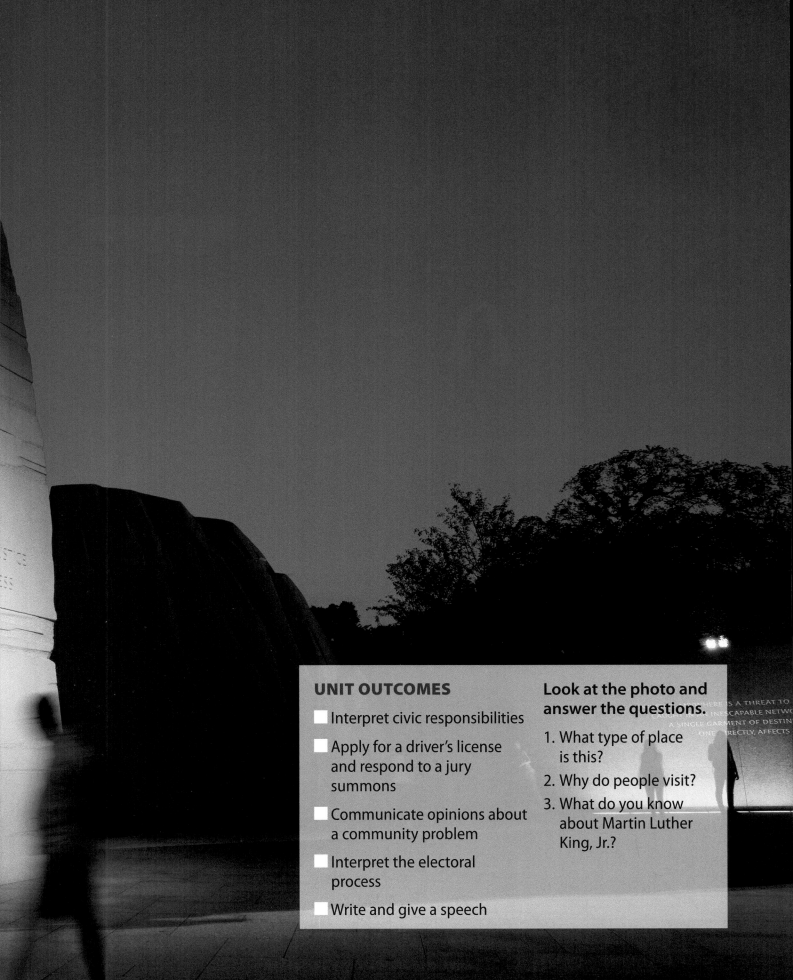

UNIT OUTCOMES

- Interpret civic responsibilities
- Apply for a driver's license and respond to a jury summons
- Communicate opinions about a community problem
- Interpret the electoral process
- Write and give a speech

Look at the photo and answer the questions.

1. What type of place is this?
2. Why do people visit?
3. What do you know about Martin Luther King, Jr.?

LESSON ① Solving problems

GOAL ▪ Interpret civic responsibilities

A. IDENTIFY Why are these things important? Complete the sentences below.

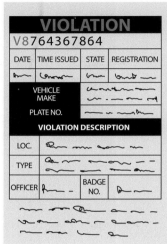

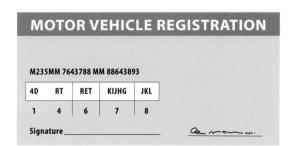

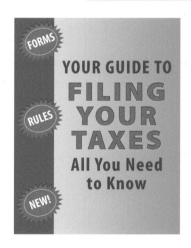

| jury summons | driver's license | ticket | car registration | taxes |

1. A _driver's license_ permits you to drive a car.

2. _Taxes_ help pay for government programs.

3. A _Car Re._ shows that you have paid to register your car with the state.

4. A _ticket_ indicates that you have violated a traffic law.

5. A _Jury Summons_ notifies you that the court needs you to appear for jury selection.

B. **SUMMARIZE** A group of students from all over the country is attending a workshop about civic responsibility in the United States. Read their conversation and see if you can define *civic responsibility* with your teacher.

Bita: I never realized how difficult it would be to get adjusted to life in the United States. There are so many things to do.

Consuela: I know. Getting a driver's license and registering my car was very complicated.

Ranjit: In New York, we have good public transportation, so I don't have to worry about a car. But I did get a jury summons the other day and I didn't know what I was supposed to do with it.

Ricardo: I got one of those last year and I couldn't understand it, so I threw it away.

Minh: You threw it away? You can't do that. You have to respond.

Bita: What about tickets? The other day, I got a ticket for jaywalking. I want to fight it, but I don't know where to go.

Ranjit: I think you have to go to court, don't you?

Minh: The most confusing thing I've had to do is pay taxes. Can't they make those forms easier to understand?

Consuela: I agree. Last year, we paid someone to do our taxes.

C. **What five situations do the students mention?**

1. 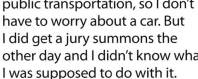 getting a driver's license

2. _____

3. _____

4. _____

5. _____

D. **RELFECT** Can you think of other situations you have had to deal with in the United States that are related to civic responsibility? Write them on the lines below.

_____

_____

_____

E. Do you have a driver's license? How did you get it? Share your experience with a group of students.

CD 1
TR 27 **F.** Bita telephones Consuela to ask how to get a driver's license. Listen to the conversation.

G. DEMONSTRATE UNDERSTANDING With a partner, ask and answer the questions based on what you learned from the conversation.

1. If I already have my driver's license from another country, do I still have to take the test?
2. How do I prepare for the written test?
3. How many questions are on the test?
4. How many questions do I have to get correct?
5. What if I don't pass it the first time?
6. What do I need to know about the driving test?
7. How do I apply for the license?
8. Do I need to make an appointment to turn in my application?
9. What do I have to do when I turn in my application?
10. How much does it cost?

H. In groups, ask and answer questions about situations related to the civic responsibilities that you listed on page 187.

Student A: Have you ever gotten a ticket before?
Student B: Yes, I got one for rolling through a stop sign.

LESSON ❷ A driver's license and jury duty

GOAL ▪ Apply for a driver's license and respond to a jury summons

A. Bita went to the DMV and got an application for a driver's license. Fill out the application.

DRIVER'S LICENSE APPLICATION

Name:

Street/PO Box:

City:	State:	Zip:

Date of Birth:	Sex: ☐ Male ☐ Female	Height:	Weight:

License Number:	Social Security No:	Restricted Code

Eye Color:
☐ Blue   ☐ Brown   ☐ Black   ☐ Green
☐ Gray   ☐ Violet   ☐ Hazel

Do you have any condition which might affect your ability to operate a motor vehicle, such as:

☐ Seizures or Unconsciousness	☐ Hearing or Vision Problem	☐ Driving Privileges Suspended
☐ Mental Disability	☐ Alcohol or Drug Problem	

***If any of the above are checked, a letter of explanation must accompany this application. Failure to do so may delay your license.**

I certify that the above statements are true. Do you wish to be an organ donor?   ☐ Yes   ☐ No

Signature:	Date:

Please check one of the following:
☐ Regular Driver's License (Class E)
☐ Out-of-State Transfer
  (Must surrender license from other state.)
 	
☐ Applicant Under Age of 18
  *Must Provide School Enrollment Form
  *License Will Expire on 21st Birthday
	DUPLICATE LICENSE FEE: $5.00
	☐ Duplicate License
	☐ Duplicate Class D License
	☐ Address change: If you move, you must change your address on your driver's license within twenty days.
	
	☐ Name Change: [＿＿＿＿＿＿＿＿＿]
	FORMER NAME
	*You must attach a copy of your marriage certificate, divorce decree, court order, or birth certificate when changing your name.

DEPARTMENT USE ONLY

Your birth certificate must be shown to the examining officer as proof of your age.
The applicant named in this application passed the examination conducted.

At ＿＿＿＿＿＿＿＿＿＿ detachment. This ＿＿＿＿＿＿＿＿ day of ＿＿＿＿＿ 20 ＿＿

Examiner   Unit Number

Restrictions ＿＿＿＿＿＿＿＿＿＿＿＿＿＿＿＿＿＿＿＿

B. **ILLUSTRATE** With a group, make a chart that explains how to get a driver's license step-by-step. Compare your chart with another group's chart.

C. **Bita and Ranjit are chatting about jury duty in the United States. Read their conversation.**

Bita: Ranjit, I just got my new driver's license in the mail!

Ranjit: Congratulations, Bita! That's wonderful.

Bita: What are you looking at?

Ranjit: Oh, I just got a jury summons in the mail. Can you tell me what I'm supposed to do with it?

Bita: Sure. I've had at least three of them.

Ranjit: What are they about anyway?

Bita: Well, in the United States, anyone accused of a crime has the right to a fair trial, which means a judge and twelve people on a jury get to listen to the case and make a decision.

Ranjit: Oh, I get it. So, can anyone be on a jury?

Bita: No, you have to meet certain qualifications.

Ranjit: Like what?

Bita: First of all, you have to be a U.S. citizen and a resident of the county or city where the trial is taking place. Also, you have to be able to understand and speak enough English to participate in the jury selection and the trial.

Ranjit: Well, I think I can speak and understand enough English, but I'm not a citizen yet. Does that disqualify me?

Bita: I'm afraid so.

Ranjit: Darn. It sounds like fun to participate in a trial. So, what do I do with this form?

Bita: There should be a series of *yes/no* questions on it. Answer each of the questions truthfully. Then, explain at the bottom why you are not qualified to participate. Some people who are citizens can be excused for other reasons, like financial hardship, medical conditions, or being older than 65. So, just fill out the form and then send it back in within ten days.

Ranjit: That's it?

Bita: That's it. Easy, huh?

D. **INFER** **Discuss the following terms with your teacher. See if you can work out their meanings using the conversation above.**

fair trial	judge	accused of a crime
jury	jury selection	qualifications

E. Read the jury summons with your teacher.

JURY SUMMONS	
Please bring this upper portion with you when you report for jury duty.	
JUROR	You are hereby notified that you have been selected for jury service in the State Trial Courts of _____ County. You are ordered to appear at the court for the following days: *May 3, 4, 5* Your Group Number: 75 Your Juror Number: 567

JUROR QUALIFICATION FORM
DETACH THIS HALF AND RETURN BY MAIL WITHIN 10 DAYS

Name:		
Address:		
City:	**State:**	**Zip:**
Home Phone:	**Date of Birth:**	
Employer:	**Occupation:**	**Work Phone:**

Answer each of the following questions under penalty of perjury.

1. Are you a citizen of the United States? ☐ yes ☐ no

2. Are you currently a resident of _____ County? ☐ yes ☐ no

3. Are you 18 years of age or older? ☐ yes ☐ no

4. Do you read, write, speak, and understand the English language?
   (If another person filled out this form, please provide their name, address, and the reasons in the space provided below.) ☐ yes ☐ no

5. Have you ever been convicted or plead guilty to theft or any felony offense? ☐ yes ☐ no

6. Do you have a physical or mental disability that would interfere with or prevent you from serving as a juror? ☐ yes ☐ no

7. Are you 65 years of age or older? ☐ yes ☐ no

If you answered NO to questions 1, 2, 3, or 4, you are automatically excused from jury duty. Please write your reason below and send in the form.

Reason I cannot serve on jury duty: _____

_____

_____

F. Fill out this jury summons with your personal information. What should you do with this form when you have filled it out?

Note: If the information is too personal, just think about the answer and don't write it in your book.

LESSON ③ Problems in your community

A. Look at the photos below and identify what these community problems might be.

B. **SOLVE** List the problems below. Discuss some possible solutions for each with a partner. Write one solution for each problem.

Problem	Solution
1.	
2.	
3.	
4.	

C. Share your solutions with the class. Vote on the best solution for each problem.

D. **Imagine you are meeting with a government official in your community. Practice the conversation below.**

Official: So, what do you think one of the biggest problems in our community is?

Resident: I think the biggest problem is <u>the number of homeless people who sleep on the street</u>.

Official: Do you have any ideas about how to solve the problem?

Resident: Actually, our neighborhood came up with two ideas. One, <u>we would like to spend our tax dollars to build a bigger homeless shelter</u>. And two, <u>we would like to put a community group together to tell the homeless people about the shelter and take them there if necessary</u>.

Official: Those are two great ideas. I'll bring them up at our next town hall meeting.

E. **GENERATE and SUGGEST** **What are some problems in your community? Work with a group to make a list. Then, come up with two possible solutions for each problem.**

Problem	Solution
1.	1. 2.
2.	1. 2.
3.	1. 2.

F. **Work with a partner to practice the conversation in Exercise D again. This time, substitute the information you wrote in Exercise E for the underlined information.**

G. BRAINSTORM Prepare to write a formal business e-mail about a problem in your community. Choose one of the problems that you have discussed with your group or a different problem in your community. Before writing the e-mail, fill in the information below.

Date: _____

Your name and address: _____

_____

Official's name and address: (Research this information.) _____

_____

State the problem: _____

_____

_____

_____

Facts or anecdotes about the problem: _____

_____

_____

_____

Suggested solutions: _____

_____

_____

Closing: _____

H. Now, write an e-mail to a local official about the community problem and your solution. Format it like a business e-mail.

L E S S O N **4** **Elections**

GOAL ▉ Interpret the electoral process

A. **The students are chatting about local elections. Read their conversation. Do you agree with them? Why is it important to understand the electoral process?**

Ranjit: Elections for a new mayor are coming up here in New York. Have any of you participated in an election before?

Bita: I haven't. I just became a U.S. citizen last year, so I will finally get to vote in this election.

Ricardo: So, if we're not citizens, we don't need to pay attention to the elections, do we?

Bita: Oh, I disagree. Even when I wasn't a citizen, I participated in local town meetings and city council meetings.

Consuela: Why?

Bita: Because I live in this community just like everyone else, and I want my voice to be heard.

Ranjit: I agree with you, Bita. I think it's important that we voice our opinions on local issues in our community. I've been listening to the candidates' speeches to see whom I would vote for. But I don't really understand how the election process works.

Bita: Let's look at the chart our teacher gave us.

B. **Read the flowchart and discuss it with your classmates and teacher.**

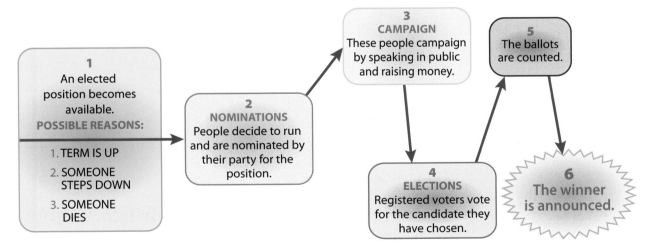

C. **CLARIFY** **Work with a partner. One of you should explain the words in the box below. The other partner should then explain the electoral process using these words. Switch roles when you have finished.**

elected	position	to step down	term
party	ballots	to announce	

D. DEMONSTRATE UNDERSTANDING Circle the best answer to each question about the electoral process.

1. When does an elected position become available?

   a. when someone's term is up

   b. when someone steps down

   c. when someone dies

   d. all of the above

2. Who nominates people to run for office?

   a. their friends and family

   b. their political party

   c. their teachers

   d. the previous elected official

3. What does it mean to campaign?

   a. vote

   b. make posters

   c. speak in public and raise money

   d. count the ballots

4. When is the winner announced?

   a. before the elections

   b. after the nominations

   c. after someone dies

   d. when all the ballots have been counted

E. Are you eligible to vote in an election? Read the list of requirements and check (✓) the ones that apply to you.

Requirements	
U.S. citizen	☐ I am a U.S. citizen.
Resident of the state you live in	☐ I am a resident.
A person who is 18 years or older	☐ I am 18 years or older.
A person who is not in jail or on parole	☐ I am not in jail or on parole.

F. If you checked all of the boxes in Exercise E, you are eligible to vote! What's the next step? You need to fill out a voter registration card. You can register to vote at these locations: a post office, a public library, the Department of Motor Vehicles (DMV), and other government offices.

G. Fill out the voter registration card.

Official Voter Registration Card

1. NAME _____

2. RESIDENCE _____

3. MAILING ADDRESS (if different from residence) _____

4. TELEPHONE NUMBER (_____) _____ - _____

5. DATE OF BIRTH _____ / _____ / _____

6. BIRTHPLACE _____

7. OCCUPATION _____

8. PRIOR REGISTRATION _____

9. POLITICAL PARTY (CHECK ONE)

☐ American Independent Party   ☐ Democratic Party   ☐ Libertarian Party

☐ Peace And Freedom Party   ☐ Republican Party   ☐ Decline To State

Other (Specify) _____

READ THIS STATEMENT BEFORE SIGNING:

I am a citizen of the United States and will be at least 18 years of age at the time of the next election. I am not imprisoned or on parole for the conviction of a felony. I certify under penalty of perjury under the laws of the state of California that the information on this affidavit is true and correct.

_____

Signature   Date

H. SUMMARIZE Write a paragraph about the electoral process. Use some of these sequencing transitions in your paragraph.

After that,	In conclusion,	First of all,	At the next stage,
In summary,	Secondly,	Next,	Finally,
Thirdly,			

LESSON ⑤ What's your platform?

GOAL ▪ Write and give a speech

🎧 **A.** Listen to the speeches from three people running for mayor of your city. For the first
CD 1
TR 28
speech, put a checkmark (✓) next to everything the candidate promises to do for
you. For the second two speeches, write down what they promise to do for you. You
will hear each speech two times.

Antonio Juliana promises to:

☐ clean up the streets

☐ lower tuition fees

☐ improve public transportation

☐ decrease gang violence

☐ get kids off the streets

☐ help the homeless people

☐ increase environmental awareness

Gary Hurt promises to:

1. clean up the beaches

2. _____

3. _____

Antonio Juliana

Gary Hurt

Kwan Tan promises to:

1. _____

2. _____

3. _____

4. _____

Kwan Tan

B. EVALUATE Who would you vote for if you were interested in...

the environment? _____

education? _____

safe streets? _____

C. Read Kwan Tan's speech.

Good evening and thank you for coming tonight! This community has given me so many opportunities and, in running for mayor, I hope to give something back to the city that welcomed me as an immigrant, educated me through my teen years, and supported me as I opened my first business.

First on my agenda is education. I will make sure your tax dollars are used to build more schools so our children won't have to sit in overcrowded classrooms. I'll lower the tuition at our community colleges so all of us will have a chance to continue and improve our education. I'll implement standards to ensure that schools are teaching our kids what they need to know. I'll start a parent-involvement program that encourages parents to participate actively in their kids' schools. Our children are the future of our community and we should invest time and money in their success.

Vote for me on Election Day and you'll have schools and a community to be proud of!

Kwan Tan for Mayor

Kwan Tan is:
- A local business owner
- A member of this community for over 25 years
- A parent of two school-age children

A vote for Kwan will ensure for our community:
- More primary and secondary schools
- Improved standards of education
- More parent involvement in schools
- Lower community college tuition

Vote for Kwan Tan

D. DEBATE What changes would Kwan like to make? Do you think these are good ideas? Discuss your opinions with a partner.

E. Study the chart with your teacher.

Passive Modals				
Example sentence	Passive subject	Modal	*Be*	Past participle
More schools *should be* built.	schools	should	be	built
Taxes *need to be* increased.	taxes	need to	be	increased
Children *must be* protected.	children	must	be	protected
Parents *have to be* involved.	parents	have to	be	involved

F. Write sentences to describe the issues Kwan Tan wants to change.

1. Kwan Tan wants to build more schools.

   She thinks that _more schools should be built_____.

2. Kwan Tan wants to lower tuition fees at community colleges.

   She says that _____.

3. Kwan Tan wants to implement standards in schools.

   She thinks that _____.

4. Kwan Tan wants to encourage parents to participate in their kids' schools.

   She believes that _____.

5. Kwan Tan wants to invest time and money in children.

   She emphasizes that _____.

G. **IDENTIFY** Think of three problems that you would like to solve in your community. Write sentences about them using passive modals.

   1. _____

   2. _____

   3. _____

H. Kwan Tan's election speech has three parts. Look for each part in her speech.

   Introduction: She introduces herself and explains why she is running for office.
   Body: She tells her audience what she plans to do if she is elected.
   Conclusion: She reminds her audience to vote and tells them once again what changes she will make to the community.

I. **DRAFT A SPEECH** Imagine that you are running for mayor of your community. How would you introduce yourself? What problems would you like to solve? Write a speech that you would give if you were running for mayor. Practice it a few times alone and then give your speech to the class.

This place looks like a garbage dump

Before You Watch

A. Look at the picture. Complete each sentence.

1. Mateo, Naomi, and Hector are at the bus _____.

2. It has a lot of trash and _____.

3. You can tell the city _____ about problems in your community.

While You Watch

B. ▶ Watch the video. Complete the dialog.

Hector: This place looks like a (1) ___*garbage dump*___.

Naomi: What a (2) _____. It used to be nice and clean.

Mateo: Well, it's definitely *not* nice and clean (3) _____.

Naomi: How did it (4) _____ so bad?

Hector: It all changed after the local (5) _____. Remember?

Mateo: That's right. After this election, I noticed that this neighborhood started to get really

(6) _____. And they stopped picking up the garbage like they used to.

Check Your Understanding

C. Read the statements. Write T for *True* or F for *False*.

1. The bus stop started looking bad just before the local elections. ___F___

2. Hector thinks that planting trees will improve the situation. _____

3. The city has been cleaning up the graffiti at the bus stop. _____

4. Naomi got 100 people to sign her letter to the city council. _____

5. Naomi, Hector, and Mateo got everything they wanted from the city. _____

Review

A. Without looking back in the unit, try to recall what you learned about each of these topics. Write notes.

Topic	I learned . . .
a jury summons	
a driver's license	
the electoral process	
voting	
giving a speech	

B. Are the statements below true or false?

	True	False
1. You have to be 18 to apply for a driver's license.	☐	☐
2. You must respond to a jury summons.	☐	☐
3. You have to be a U.S. citizen to serve on a jury.	☐	☐
4. You don't have to speak English to serve on a jury trial.	☐	☐
5. People who want to run for office must be nominated.	☐	☐
6. Anyone who lives in the United States can vote.	☐	☐
7. You can register to vote at the DMV.	☐	☐
8. Only U.S. citizens can get involved in the community.	☐	☐

C. What are three problems in your community that you would like to solve? How would you solve them? Work with a small group to fill in the chart.

Problem	Solution
1.	
2.	
3.	

Learner Log

I can identify community problems and solutions.   I can communicate opinions about community issues.
■ Yes   ■ Maybe   ■ No   ■ Yes   ■ Maybe   ■ No

D. **There are six steps in the electoral process. Number them in the correct order.**

_____ Ballots are counted.

_____ Elections are held.

_____ Candidates campaign.

_____ Candidates are nominated.

_____ The winner is announced.

_____ A position becomes available.

E. **What are the four requirements to be eligible to vote? List them below.**

1. _____

2. _____

3. _____

4. _____

F. **What are three places where you can register to vote? List them below.**

1. _____

2. _____

3. _____

G. **Rewrite each sentence using a passive modal.**

1. We must protect the environment.

   _____

2. They should reduce our taxes.

   _____

3. They need to invest money in our education system.

   _____

4. They need to build more public transportation.

   _____

5. We should protect our children from gang violence.

   _____

Learner Log

I can interpret and explain the electoral process.   I can write and give a speech.
☐ Yes ☐ Maybe ☐ No   ☐ Yes ☐ Maybe ☐ No

H.   Imagine that you are running for mayor. What are your solutions for the following problems?

1. Problem: gang violence

   Solution: _____

   _____

2. Problem: traffic

   Solution: _____

   _____

3. Problem: residents not using public transportation

   Solution: _____

   _____

4. Problem: homeless children

   Solution: _____

   _____

I.   Go back through your book and make a list of all the vocabulary strategies you learned. Check (✓) the strategies that are the most useful to you.

	Vocabulary Strategies I Have Learned

Conduct an election

With a team, you will prepare a candidate for an election. As a class, you will conduct an election.

1. **COLLABORATE** Form a campaign committee with four or five students. Choose positions for each member of your team.

Position	Job description	Student name
Student 1: **Campaign Director**	Check that everyone speaks English and participates.	
Student 2: **Speech Writer**	Write candidate's speech.	
Student 3: **Candidate**	Give speech to class.	
Students 4/5: **Spokespeople**	Announce nomination. Introduce candidate. Create ballot.	

2. With your group, decide who will be running for school president. Announce the nomination to the class.

3. As a class, create a ballot with all the nominees' names on it. Make a ballot box for students to put their ballots in after they vote.

4. With your group, decide what issues are most important and write a campaign speech.

5. Candidates give speeches to the class.

6. Students all vote.

7. The teacher counts the ballots and announces the winner.

EXPLORERS SOL GUY AND JOSH THOME

Social Change and Storytelling

"Mainstream media has grown stagnant; today's youth are thirsty for new, meaningful ideas."
—Josh Thome

A. Read about some of the episodes in the 4REAL TV Series, Season 1. What do you think the purpose of this TV series is?

1. Mos Def rolls into Rio's infamous City Of God, where Brazil's #1 rap artist, MV Bill, shows how his program empowers favela youth through the art of hip hop.

2. UK rapper/artist M.I.A. learns about the work of child rights leader Kimmie Weeks. They visit with Liberian President Ellen Johnson Sirleaf, fix a playground, and throw a block party in Monrovia.

3. Hip hop star K'naan travels to Kenya's Kibera, the largest slum in East Africa. There, he connects with local hero, Salim Mohamed, who runs a medical clinic and a soccer program for over 4,000 kids.

4. In the hills of Haiti, Flea of Red Hot Chili Peppers and 4REAL host Sol Guy meet rural health aide Camseuze Moise, who provides medical care and health education to thousands of people.

B. IDENTIFY What are the social problems listed in the episodes above? Write a list in your notebook.

EXAMPLE: _young people getting into trouble_

C. **Read about the work that Sol Guy and Josh Thome do.**

Sol Guy and Josh Thome are storytellers, and they have important stories to tell. There is a group in South Africa who wrote a hit song and lowered the AIDS rate in their region. Someone left a baby in a box and that baby grew up to run a medical clinic in a slum in East Africa. There is a boy who was trained as a child soldier and survived civil war in Liberia and now builds orphanages and playgrounds for youth in his country. These are just three of the stories they have to tell.

Sol and Josh were childhood friends who went to school together in the Kootenay mountains of British Columbia. Their parents taught them how important it is to be socially responsible. They went their separate ways after high school, but reconnected after living two separate lives filled with experiences that deeply affected them. These experiences led them to eventually create 4REAL, a TV series that would tell the stories of social and economic progress around the world.

What makes their series unique is that they get TV, film, and music stars to be part of the documentary, traveling all over the world to help them tell the stories. Each episode goes on an adventure to a different part of the world and highlights a young leader who is doing extraordinary things. To show their appreciation, Sol and Josh donate 50% of the profits from the TV series back to the young leaders to continue the great work they are doing.

Sol and Josh want to show young people how they can positively affect change by being proactive in the world. "Youth have always been a key force in creating change. This generation has so much potential—we want to help them see that it's actually cool to care."

D. **SUPPOSE** **Imagine you are going to create an episode for 4REAL. Think of a social problem in your community and someone who is doing something about it. Who would you highlight?**

Person: _____

Social problem: _____

What this person is doing about it: _____

_____

E. **Reread the last quote in the reading. What are some ways you could show the youth in your community that it is "cool to care"? Make a list with a group.**

1. _____

2. _____

3. _____

▶ VIDEO CHALLENGE

Searching for Genghis Khan

Before You Watch

A. **Look at the map. Then, read each question. Choose the answer you think is the best.**

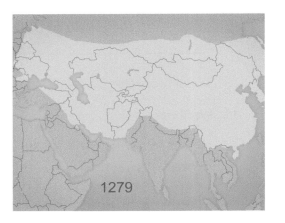

1. What part of the world does the light area on the map show?

   a. North America   b. South America

   c. Asia   d. Africa

2. What countries do you think are inside the light gray area?

   a. Mongolia and China   b. Mexico and Canada

   c. Egypt and India   d. Japan and Vietnam

3. What do you think the number *1279* means?

   a. number of people   b. year   c. size of the region   d. number of countries

B. Look at the picture. Choose the best caption for the picture and write it on the line.

1. About 60 percent of the world's population lives in Asia.

2. Genghis Khan—leader of the largest empire in history

3. Mongolia is a large country in east-central Asia.

4. The Mongols are people from the country of Mongolia.

_____

C. Complete each sentence in the timeline with the correct word from the box.

search	look for
troops	a group of soldiers
warrior	a soldier who shows great skills
empire	a large number of countries with one ruler
crowdsourcing	getting money, services, or ideas from people in an online community
tomb	a special building to put someone who is dead; can be under or above ground

1. **1206** Genghis Khan builds a strong army that has many _____.

2. **1209** Genghis Khan becomes a _____ and fights against China.

3. **1227** Genghis Kahn dies and his people hide his body in a secret _____.

4. **1279** Genghis Khan's _____ becomes the largest in the world.

5. **2008** Dr. Albert Lin begins his _____ for Genghis Khan.

6. **2010** Dr. Albert Lin uses _____ to get people from all over the world to help him study maps.

While You Watch

D. Watch the video and listen. Check the information about Dr. Albert Yu-Min Lin. Write T for *True* or F for *False*.

_____ 1. He works at a university in California.

_____ 2. He rides horses.

_____ 3. He is a teacher.

_____ 4. He is an engineer.

_____ 5. He is Chinese.

_____ 6. His family is from Japan.

E. **Watch the video and listen. Then, match the picture with the correct description.**

_____ 1. These are Mongolian houses.

_____ 2. Dr. Lin uses satellite technology.

_____ 3. Dr. Lin is looking for Genghis Khan's tomb.

_____ 4. This is Dr. Lin and his research team in Mongolia.

_____ 5. This is the beginning of the Mongol Empire.

_____ 6. People think Genghis Khan's tomb is in this area.

F. Watch the video and listen again. Circle the correct answer.

1. What does Dr. Lin call the people from crowdsourcing who help him?

    a. citizen scientists   b. young explorers   c. skilled researchers

2. What is Dr. Lin's job for *National Geographic*?

    a. photographer   b. explorer   c. writer

3. What is the name of the capital city of Mongolia?

    a. Ulaanbatar   b. Tokyo   c. Beijing

4. What is the name of the area where people think Genghis Khan's tomb is?

    a. Warrior's Home   b. Mongolian Tomb   c. the Forbidden Zone

5. What do the people from crowdsourcing use to help Dr. Lin?

    a. maps   b. books   c. pictures

After You Watch

sacred	something or someone people think of as more special than anything or anyone else
cutting edge	the newest and the best there is
unified	many parts put together
leader	a powerful person who other people follow
citizen scientist	a person who gives time and resources to help scientists explore or research

G. Some people believe that Genghis Khan's tomb is in *No Man's Land*. What do you think this name means? Why does it have that name? Discuss as a class.

> *No Man's Land* means no one can visit there.

H. What is the reason Dr. Albert Lin uses *crowdsourcing* to find Genghis Kahn's tomb? Discuss as a class.

> Dr. Albert Lin doesn't want to do any damage to places.

STAND OUT VOCABULARY LIST

rest area 95
scenic 95
sign up 86
structures 99
suggestion 93
volunteer 98

UNIT 5
ache 117
advise 128
allergy 128
announce 122
arthritis 128
asthma 128
calculate 116
calories 123
cancer 128
carbohydrates 123
chiropractor 121
cholesterol 120
circulatory 128
colon 128
common cold 117
co-pay 126
cough 117
coverage 126
deductible 126
dentist 121
dependants 127
diabetes 128
digestive system 128
emotional 128
examine 119
fat 123
fiber 123
flu 117
health care
    professional 122
healthy 114
hernia 128
high blood pressure 128
ingredients 123
intestinal 128
joint 128
junk food 120
kidney 128

liver 128
meditating 115
mental 128
mental health 115
muscle spasm 117
muscular 128
nutrients 124
obstetrician 121
optometrist 118
overweight 124
physical health 115
pediatrician 121
percentage 116
physical health 115
podiatrist 121
poll 116
premium 126
prescription plan 126
protein 123
providers 126
puzzles 115
reproductive organs 128
reputation 126
respiratory 128
saturated fat 123
serving size 123
sodium 123
spouse 127
stroke 128
throwing up 117
thyroid 128
ulcer 128
unhealthy 114
vitamins 123

UNIT 6
appearance 151
appropriateness 151
benefit (v) 150
benefits (n) 141
certificate 144
characteristics 139
conflict 150
cover letter 147
criteria 152
degree 145

effectiveness 151
eye contact 151
facial expressions 151
identify 147
impression 152
interests 140
job responsibilities 139
job titles 139
key strengths 147
mock 152
overtime 141
posture 151
required qualifications 141
resume 145
self-confidence 151
skill 138
strength 150
troubleshooting 144
voice level 151
weakness 150
willingness 151

UNIT 7
active 166
appropriate 162
brochure 166
Census Bureau data 175
close the gap 175
construction 168
contributions to the
    company 175
counterpart 175
cover your bases 175
deserve 176
document 175
door frames 168
ethical 171
ethics 171
flowchart 169
get someone's
    attention 168
hesitate 174
inappropriate 162
lumber 168
misunderstanding 165
pardon me 168

passive 166
politely 168
raise 175
rehearse 175
relevant 172
review 175
shipment 168
solution 169
star performer 175
tag 163

UNIT 8
accused of a crime 190
anecdotes 194
announce 195
ballots 195
campaign 195
car registration 186
case 190
civic responsibility 186
disqualify 190
elected 195
eligible 196
environmental
    awareness 198
fair trial 190
gang violence 198
homeless 198
homeless shelter 193
jaywalking 187
judge 190
jury 190
jury selection 190
jury summons 186
local official 194
mental disability 191
overcrowded
    freeway 192
position 195
public transportation 187
qualifications 190
step down 195
taxes 186
term 195
ticket 186
tuition 198

STAND OUT IRREGULAR VERB LIST

The following verbs are used in *Stand Out* and have irregular past tense forms.

Base Form	Simple Past	Past Participle
be	was, were	been
become	became	become
begin	began	begun
break	broke	broken
bring	brought	brought
build	built	built
buy	bought	bought
catch	caught	caught
come	came	come
do	did	done
drink	drank	drunk
drive	drove	driven
eat	ate	eaten
fall	fell	fallen
feel	felt	felt
fight	fought	fought
find	found	found
fly	flew	flown
get	got	gotten
give	gave	given
go	went	gone
grow	grew	grown
have	had	had
hear	heard	heard
hold	held	held
hurt	hurt	hurt
keep	kept	kept
know	knew	known
learn	learned	learned/learnt
lend	lent	lent

Base Form	Simple Past	Past Participle
lose	lost	lost
make	made	made
mean	meant	meant
meet	met	met
pay	paid	paid
put	put	put
read	read	read
ride	rode	ridden
run	ran	run
say	said	said
sell	sold	sold
send	sent	sent
set	set	set
show	showed	showed/shown
sit	sat	sat
sleep	slept	slept
speak	spoke	spoken
spend	spent	spent
spread	spread	spread
stand	stood	stood
steal	stole	stolen
take	took	taken
teach	taught	taught
tell	told	told
think	thought	thought
throw	threw	thrown
wake	woke	woken
wear	wore	worn
win	won	won
write	wrote	written

STAND OUT GRAMMAR REFERENCE

Used to	
Example	**Rule**
Minh *used to* go to school during the day. Bita *used to* be an architect in Iran.	**Affirmative:** *used to* + base verb
Bita *did not use to* go to school at night. Minh *didn't use to* take care of his grandchildren.	**Negative:** *did* + *not (didn't)* + *use to* + base verb **Incorrect:** ~~I didn't used to go to school.~~
Did Minh *use to* work? *Did* Bita *use to* study English?	**Yes/No Question:** *did* + subject + *use to* + base verb **Incorrect:** ~~Did Bita used to live in Iran?~~
Where *did* Minh *use to* work? What *did* Bita *use to* study?	**Wh- Question:** *wh-* word + *did* + subject + *use to* + base verb
Used to + base verb expresses a past habit or state which is now different.	

Future Tense Using *Will*	
Example	**Rule**
In the spring of 2009, *I will ask* my boss for a raise. In the summer, *I will look* for a job.	Future tense = *will* + base verb
In spoken English, people often use contractions: I will = *I'll*.	

Adjective Clauses		
Main clause (Subject clause)	**Relative pronoun**	**Adjective clause**
This is the place	**where**	I grew up.
She is the person	**who (that)**	influenced me most.
A journal is something	**which (that)**	can help you focus on important things.
Main clause (Object clause)	**Relative pronoun**	**Adjective clause**
This is the woman	**who (whom)**	I met yesterday.
Here is the book	**which**	you gave me this morning.
Adjectival clauses describe a preceding noun. They can describe a subject noun or an object noun. If the noun is an object, you can leave out the relative pronoun.		

Contrary-to-Fact Conditionals

Condition (*if* + past tense verb)	Result (*would* + base verb)
If she *got* a raise,	she *would buy* a new house.
If they *didn't spend* so much money on rent,	they *would have* more money for entertainment.
If I *were* a millionaire,	I *would give* all my money to charity.
If John *weren't* so busy at work,	he *would spend* more time with his children.

- *Contrary-to-fact* (or *unreal*) *conditional statements* are sentences that are not true.
- The *if*-clause can come in the first or second part of the sentence. Notice how commas are used in the examples. (If you reverse the order of the condition and result clauses, omit the comma.)
- In written English, use *were* (instead of was) for *if*-clauses with first and third person singular forms of *be*.
- In spoken English, people often use contractions: I would = *I'd*; she would = *she'd*, etc.

Contrary-to-Fact Questions

Wh- Question	*Yes/No* Question
What + *would* + subject + base verb + *if* + subject + past tense	*Would* + subject + base verb + *if* + subject + past tense
What would you do *if* you won the lottery?	*Would* you give up your job *if* you won the lottery?

Passive Voice: Present Tense

Subject	*Be*	Past Participle		Explanation
Ads	are	written	to sell products.	Since we know that ads are written by advertisers, the information "by advertisers" is not important.
The camera	is	advertised	on television.	Since we know that the store is advertising the camera, the information "by the store" is not important.

We use the passive voice to emphasize the object of the action or when the doer is not important.

Questions Using Comparative and Superlative Adjectives

Question word	Subject	Verb	Adjective or Noun	Rule
Which	one place house	is	bigger? closer to work? the safest?	Use *be* when following the verb with an adjective.
		has	more rooms? the biggest floor plan?	Use *have* before a noun.

Long and Short Answers

Question	Short answer	Long answer	Rules
Which one is bigger, the condominium or the house?	The condominium.	The condominium is bigger. The condominium is bigger than the house.	• When talking about two things and mentioning both of them, use *than*.
Which place has more rooms?	The house.	The house has more rooms. The house has more rooms than the condominium.	• When talking about two things, but only mentioning one of them, do not use *than*.

Yes/No Questions and Answers

Do you want	air-conditioning? a backyard?	Yes, I do. No, I don't.
Do they need	a balcony? a garage?	Yes, they do. No, they don't.
Does the house have	heating? a pool?	Yes, it does. No, it doesn't.

Information Questions

Information	Example questions		
type of property	What type	of property	do you want? is it?
number of bathrooms number of bedrooms	How many	bedrooms bathrooms	do you want? does it have?
location	Where		is it?
price range	What		is your price range?
down payment (percentage)	How much		can you put down?

Embedded Questions

Introductory question	Embedded question	Rules
Can you show me	where *Orange Avenue is*?	In an embedded information question, the subject comes before the verb.
Do you know	if there is a library near here?	For *yes/no* questions, use *if* before the embedded question.
Can you tell me	when the library opens?	For questions with *do* or *does*, take out *do/does* and use the verb that agrees with the subject.

Why do we use embedded questions? They sound more polite than direct questions.

Present Perfect Continuous

Example	Form
I *have been resting* for three hours.	*Affirmative sentence*: has/have + *been* + present participle
He *hasn't been sleeping* well recently.	*Negative sentence*: has/have + *not* + *been* + present participle
How *long have they lived/have they been living* here?	*Question*: has/have + subject + *been* + present participle

- To emphasize the duration of an activity or state that started in the past and continues in the present. Example: The president *has been sleeping* since 9 A.M.
- To show that an activity has been in progress recently. Example: You*'ve been going* to the doctor a lot lately.
- With some verbs (*work, live, teach*), there is no difference in meaning between the present perfect simple and the present perfect continuous. Example: They *have lived/have been living* here since 2000.

Note: Some verbs are not usually used in the continuous form. These include *be, believe, hate, have, know, like,* and *want.*

Present Perfect Simple

Example	Form
He *has seen* the doctor. I have moved four times in my life.	*Affirmative sentence*: has/have + past participle
They *haven't been* to the hospital to see her.	*Negative sentence*: has/have + *not* + past participle OR has/have + *never* + past participle
Have you *written* to your mother?	*Question*: has/have + subject + past participle

- When something happened (or didn't happen) at an unspecified time in the past. Example: She *has* never *broken* her arm.
- When something happened more than once in the past (and could possibly happen again in the future). Example: I *have moved* four times in my life.
- When something started at a specific time in the past and continues in the present. Example: They *have lived* here for ten years.

Direct Speech	Indirect Speech	Rule
"You have to exercise more."	The doctor *explained* (that) I had to exercise more.	- Change pronoun. - Change present tense to past tense.
"The most important thing is your health."	The doctor *said* (that) the most important thing was my health.	

Direct Speech	Indirect Speech
I want to lose weight. My test results are negative.	I told *you* (that) I wanted to lose weight. He notified *me* (that) my test results were negative.
It is important to check your heart rate. I feel sick.	My personal trainer said (that) it was important to check my heart rate. She complained (that) she felt sick.

- Some verbs are usually followed by an indirect object or pronoun. (*tell, assure, advise, convince, notify, promise, remind, teach, warn*)
- Some verbs are NOT followed by an indirect object or pronoun. (*say, agree, announce, answer, complain, explain, reply, state*)

Tag Questions

Positive statement	Tag	Negative statement	Tag
She works,	doesn't she?	She doesn't work,	does she?
She is working,	isn't she?	She isn't working,	is she?
She worked,	didn't she?	She didn't work,	did she?
She will work,	won't she?	She won't work,	will she?
She is going to work,	isn't she?	She isn't going to work,	is she?
She has worked,	hasn't she?	She hasn't worked,	has she?
She had worked,	hadn't she?	She hadn't worked,	had she?

Passive Voice

Example sentence	Passive subject	*Be*	Past participle	(*by* + person or thing)
The note was written by Jim.	It	was	written	by Jim
The orders were sent yesterday. (We don't know who sent them.)	They	were	sent	

- Use the passive voice to emphasize the object of the action, or when the doer of the action is unknown or unimportant.
- To change an active sentence into a passive sentence, switch the subject and the object, and change the verb to the correct tense of *be* + the past participle. The word *by* is used before the doer of the action.

Passive Modals

Example sentence	Passive subject	Modal	*Be*	Past participle
More schools *should be* built.	schools	should	be	built
Taxes *need to be* increased.	taxes	need to	be	increased
Children *must be* protected.	children	must	be	protected
Parents *have to be* involved.	parents	have to	be	involved

PHOTO CREDITS

STAND OUT SKILLS INDEX

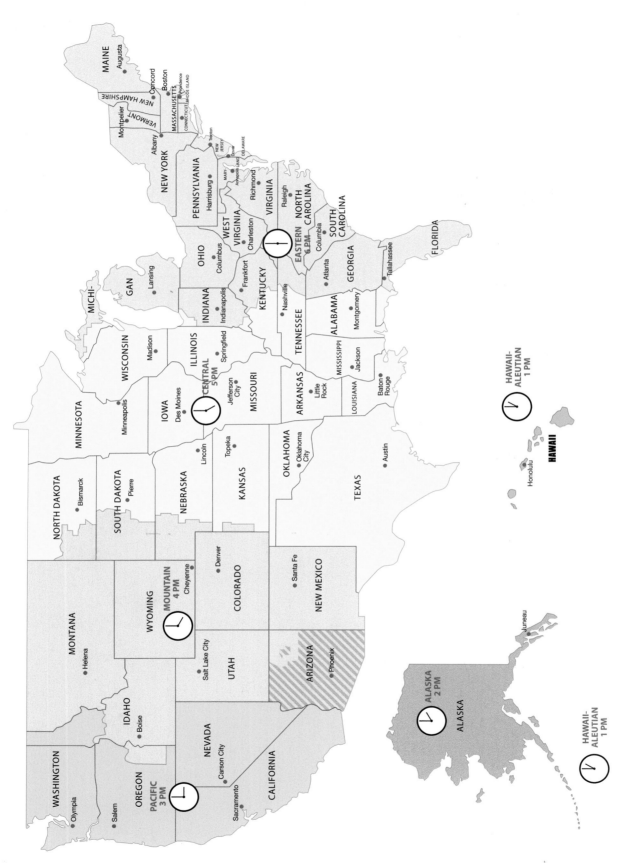